bistro

Dedicated to Tony Waller, 1952–2003.

acknowledgments

A heartfelt thanks to Tracey Rayner for her unflagging support, and to Ian White for the wonderful wine suggestions.

Published by Murdoch Books Pty Limited

AUSTRALIA
Murdoch Books® Australia
Pier 8/9
23 Hickson Road
Millers Point NSW 2000
Phone: (612) 8220 2000
Fax: (612) 8220 2558

UK
Murdoch Books UK Ltd
Erico House, 6th Floor North
93–99 Upper Richmond Road
Putney, London SW15 2TG
Phone: + 44 (0) 20 8785 5995
Fax: + 44 (0) 20 8785 5985

Chief executive: Juliet Rogers
Publisher: Kay Scarlett

Creative director and concept: Marylouise Brammer
Project manager: Margaret Malone
Photographer: Prue Ruscoe
Stylist: Sarah DeNardi
Editor: Justine Harding
Designer: Annette Fitzgerald
Food preparation: Jo Glynn
Extra photography: Jared Fowler (cover and pages 8 and 11)
Production: Monika Paratore
Editorial director: Diana Hill

National Library of Australia Cataloguing-in-Publication Data
Johnson, Philip, 1959-
Bistro.
Includes index.
ISBN 1 74045 383 2.
1. Cookery, French. I. Title
641.5944

Text © Philip Johnson 2004. Design and photography © Murdoch Books® 2004.
Printed by Toppan Printing Hong Kong Co. Ltd. PRINTED IN CHINA. First printed 2004.

Notes: Those at risk from the effects of salmonella food poisoning (including the elderly, pregnant women and children) should consult their GP with any concerns about eating raw eggs.
We have used 20 ml tablespoon measures. If you are using a 15 ml tablespoon, for most recipes the difference will not be noticeable. However, for recipes using small amounts of flour and cornflour, add an extra teaspoon for each tablespoon specified.

The publisher would like to thank the following for their generosity in supplying furniture, props and kitchenware for this book: Chee Soon and Fitzgerald; The Bay Tree; Crave; Major and Tom; Orrefors Kosta Boda; Porters Paints and Mud Australia. Special thanks to Waterford Wedgewood and Villeroy & Boch for their beautiful plates, glassware and cutlery; to Sarah Dale from the Ceramic shed for specially producing items for the book and to Michael Whitney and Allison Davies at Thonet for the use of their gorgeous chairs.

bistro

that perfect place just around the corner

philip johnson

MURDOCH BOOKS

contents

origins

There have been several theories on the origin of the word bistro, and the one I found to be particularly charming is from 1815, when Russian soldiers marched into Paris following the defeat of Napoleon at Waterloo. The starving soldiers ran into the café and bars shouting 'Bistro! Bistro!' Which, simply translated, means 'Quick! Quick!'

While this may be more fable than fact, without any doubt it was Paris in the early 1800s that saw the emergence of the first bistros. These popular cafés were generally situated in the city's many market areas, and catered mainly to the working class. They were located where people could easily meet for a coffee or a glass of wine. Soon, almost every neighbourhood had their own bistro, and workers, artists and intellectuals would eat alongside one another, all attracted by the reliable and inexpensive fare offered in unpretentious surroundings.

Since those early days, bistros have been in and out of favour, but today, they are as popular as ever. Bistro cooking may not be haute cuisine, but that is not necessarily a bad thing. Uncomplicated cooking can produce equally delicious fare. As well, the atmosphere, the essence of the original bistros, has made a return. In a traditional bistro, every available seat was used, and if someone dined alone, he or she might have been seated at the bar or next to a complete stranger. Even the owner of the bistro would be seen carrying plates from the kitchen to the hungry patrons.

It is this feel-good atmosphere, this sharing of a satisfying meal with family, friends or an acquaintance that is, and always has been, a cherished part of life — and what makes the bistro so special. It is this belief that encouraged me to create my own bistro, which I did, in 1995, when I opened my restaurant, e'cco.

é'cco

sed bistro

my bistro

I often recall a remark made by a prominent Brisbane chef following his first dining experience at my restaurant, e'cco. He commented that my food wasn't really 'bistro' food, and this was meant as a compliment in that my food was far more sophisticated than 'normal' bistro food (a point I believe to be subjective and debatable). If this is the case, then I make no apologies for attention to detail. In my view, the essence of a bistro is a simplistic, no-nonsense, almost austere environment — no tablecloths, relaxed yet efficient service by staff who dress down rather than up and food that is honest, wholesome and full of flavour. I think we succeed in all these areas.

Following the sale of my first establishment, quite a formal, labour-intensive French restaurant, I longed for a change of pace and style. I returned to London, having worked there previously, and ventured into a bistro that immediately presented me with a working model for my cooking, which was to become the inspiration behind e'cco. But it was in France that I fully appreciated the unique pleasure of a traditional bistro. Accompanied by my wife, Shirley, I travelled to Languedoc to discover Béziers, a picturesque French town on the Orb River. I wandered into my first true bistro and was instantly smitten. It was just as I had imagined — located in the town square and a hive of activity, bustling with communal and smaller tables, and unforgettable with the noise of people enjoying the food while talking business, sport and politics.

I can't recall the exact menu, although there was a blackboard displaying offerings such as pâtés, terrines, rillettes and soup to start, more substantial fare such as coq au vin and veal stew to follow, and desserts such as lemon tart and tarte tatin to finish. Realizing we weren't locals, one of the waiters, en route to another table, paused to show us some of the dishes. It was a fantastic gesture, a brilliant show-and-tell in true French style. We finished our meal and were so captivated by the environment that we didn't want to leave.

It was at that moment that I knew what direction my next restaurant would take. It would be everything I had just experienced. Firstly, a space that made the clientele feel welcome and at ease. Secondly, casually-attired staff who were friendly, well informed and efficient. And thirdly, although not French bistro, food that would be my interpretation of bistro food. Food that had flavour above all else, but also had visual appeal. Food that hadn't been played with or fussed over, yet delivered maximum appeal on the plate. Real food, honest food, using the best local produce — and at the right price. I didn't want a special occasion restaurant or one that was only full on a Saturday night. If people are able to visit regularly, there will be a nice ambience.

I have never strayed far from my original ideas and beliefs. One significant difference is that the menu is constantly evolving. My clientele like variety, they like change. I think it would be much harder to stay with the same menu as is commonplace in Europe. The key is to evolve, but to show restraint — people want to at least see a common thread through the menu when they return, not the slate wiped clean.

bistro cooking at home

So how does this translate into a collection of recipes? The recipes are a mix of ones that would be at home in a French bistro and others that reflect the wonderful variety of produce available in Australia, but all adhere to my core approach to cooking. Like all good bistros, there are a variety of dishes: you may want to cook only a light salad or soup, or you may want something substantial and rich to serve at a special meal. Of course, you may also want to head straight to desserts, with a glass of wine to accompany you, and that is fine by me. Many are simple to prepare; some are not — but think of them as a challenge. If bistro dining is all about ambience, simplicity and real food, then I hope these are the recipes that allow you to create that experience in your own home. So here it is — my take on bistro cooking and eating. Now go and cook, your friends are waiting!

Philip Johnson

classic beginnings

It's a strange phenomenon, but it's always the simplest dish that draws the most praise.

pacific oysters with leek and champagne sabayon

36 Pacific oysters
1 tablespoon unsalted butter
3 leeks, white part only, thinly sliced
3 egg yolks

a good splash of Champagne or white wine (about
    80 ml/2^1/$_2$ fl oz/^{1}/$_3$ cup)
salmon roe, herring roe or caviar

Serves 6

Shuck and strain the oysters, reserving any liquid. Return the oysters to their shells. Heat the butter in a large frying pan. Sauté the leek with some salt and freshly ground black pepper, without colouring, until tender. Set aside to cool to room temperature.

Put the egg yolks, oyster liquid, a good splash of Champagne and a good pinch of salt and freshly ground black pepper in a heatproof bowl. Sit the bowl over a large saucepan of boiling water and whisk until the mixture has doubled in volume. To serve, arrange six oysters on each serving plate and top with the sautéed leek. Spoon the Champagne sabayon and roe over the leek. Alternatively, before adding the roe, you can glaze the oysters under a hot grill (broiler) for a few minutes until golden.

to drink
Wairau River Sauvignon Blanc, Marlborough, New Zealand
Freshly shucked oysters and a crisp sauvignon blanc; they could have been created with the other in mind.

bloody mary oyster shooters

6 x ^{1}/$_2$ nip (15 ml/^{1}/$_2$ fl oz) vodka
6 rock oysters, shucked, cleaned and removed from
    the shells
150 ml (5 fl oz) tomato juice

Worcestershire sauce, to taste
Tabasco sauce, to taste
^{1}/$_2$ lemon

Makes 6

Pour ^{1}/$_2$ nip of vodka into each of six shot glasses. Add an oyster to each glass. Fill the glasses with the tomato juice, then add a dash of Worcestershire and a small drop of Tabasco, to taste. Squeeze a little lemon juice over the top. Finish with a grind of black pepper.

to drink
Zubrowka Bison Grass Vodka
Pure Polish potato vodka infused with bison grass — its underlying character of green tea cuts through the spicy richness of the tomato.

steamed mussels provençale

I nearly always have mussels on my menus as they are one of those unique foods that have so much natural flavour that they inevitably make you, the cook, look good!

2 kg (4 lb 8 oz) black mussels, cleaned,
   beards removed
2 tablespoons olive oil
2 teaspoons crushed garlic
750 ml (26 fl oz/3 cups) white wine
3 tomatoes, diced
a handful of flat-leaf (Italian) parsley, leaves picked,
   washed and roughly chopped
lemon wedges, to serve

Serves 6

Discard any mussels that are broken or cracked or do not close when tapped.

Heat half the olive oil in a large saucepan over high heat. Sauté half the garlic, without colouring, add half the mussels and stir well. Add half the wine, half the tomato and half the parsley. Stir to combine. Cover and cook for 2–3 minutes, or until the mussels open. Discard any mussels that do not open. Repeat the process with the remaining ingredients.

To serve, carefully lift the mussels into serving bowls, spoon over some of the tomato sauce and serve with lemon wedges.

note
The saucepan should be large enough to hold the mussels comfortably. Cook the mussels in two batches or the heat will drop considerably, inhibiting some of the mussels from opening. Either use two large saucepans or remove the first batch once cooked, with its sauce, and keep warm.

to drink
Lake Breeze Langhorne Creek Grenache, South Australia
The intense aromas of pepper and raspberry complement the sweet maritime tomato base.

peking duck salad wrapped in rice paper

1 Chinese roasted duck (see note)
1/4 Chinese cabbage (wong bok), shredded
50 g (1 3/4 oz/1/2 cup) bean shoots
a small handful of Vietnamese mint, leaves picked
   and washed
a small handful of mint, leaves picked and washed
a handful of coriander (cilantro), leaves picked
   and washed
3 spring onions (scallions), sliced on the diagonal
1 medium red chilli, seeded and thinly
   sliced lengthwise

85 g (3 oz/1/2 cup) roasted unsalted cashews, chopped
25 g (1 3/4 oz/1/4 cup) Asian fried shallots
1 tablespoon sesame seeds, roasted
12 sheets of round rice paper wrappers, 20 cm
   (8 inches) in diameter

Dressing
60 ml (2 fl oz/1/4 cup) hoisin sauce
60 ml (2 fl oz/1/4 cup) soy sauce
90 g (3 1/4 oz/1/4 cup) honey

Makes 12

Remove the meat from the duck and slice it into thin, uniform strips.

To make the dressing, whisk the hoisin sauce, soy sauce and honey until combined.

Gently toss the Chinese cabbage, bean shoots, herbs, spring onion, chilli, cashews, fried shallots and sesame seeds together in a large bowl. Add the duck meat and enough dressing to moisten the salad.

Fill a flat tray with cold water. Put two to three sheets of rice paper in the water to soften for a few minutes. Gently lift the rice paper sheets onto a clean, damp towel, one at a time. Put spoonfuls of the duck salad at the base of each sheet and wrap up tightly. Repeat with the remaining rice paper and duck salad. If the rolls are made slightly in advance, cover them with a clean damp cloth until ready to serve. Serve any leftover dressing alongside as a dipping sauce.

note
Chinese roasted duck can be bought from Chinatown food stores.
When wrapping the rolls, don't be afraid to vary the size and shape. They can either be wrapped similar to a spring roll, or folded so that some of the salad is visible.

to drink
Moscow Mule
The ultimate party ice-breaker: Peking duck rolls accompanied by a Moscow mule. To make, build 60–90 ml (2–3 1/4 fl oz) vodka, the juice of 1/2 a lime and a twist of lime zest in a tall glass over ice. Top up with ginger beer.

chermoula-spiced prawns

Chermoula is a Moroccan spice traditionally served with fish, but it's fantastic with poultry as well. Don't be afraid to adjust the heat of the spices to suit your own taste.

18–24 large raw prawns (shrimp), peeled and
   deveined, tails intact
lime quarters, to serve

Chermoula
1 tablespoon cumin seeds, roasted
1 tablespoon coriander seeds, roasted
2 tablespoons sweet paprika
2 teaspoons cayenne pepper, or to taste
a pinch of saffron threads
2 teaspoons sea salt
1 teaspoon ground black pepper
125 ml (4 fl oz/$1/2$ cup) olive oil

Serves 6

To make the chermoula, use a mortar and pestle to grind the cumin seeds, coriander seeds, paprika, cayenne pepper, saffron threads, sea salt and black pepper to a fine powder. (Alternatively, blend the spices briefly in a small food processor or coffee grinder.) Transfer the spice powder to a bowl and whisk in the olive oil.

Add the prepared prawns to the bowl and toss to combine well with the chermoula. Cover and refrigerate the prawns overnight.

Preheat a barbecue chargrill or ridged grill pan. Drain the excess oil from the prawns. Barbecue or grill the prawns until they are just cooked. Serve with the lime quarters to squeeze over the prawns.

to drink
Brown Brothers Pinot Grigio, Victoria
Spicy, robust North African spices and rich, mouth filling pinot grigio — a great barbecue match.

salt-and-pepper squid with roast chilli sauce

1.2 kg (2 lb 11 oz) medium-sized squid
125 g (4^1/$_2$ oz/1 cup) plain (all-purpose) flour
sea salt
oil, for deep-frying
a handful of coriander (cilantro), leaves picked
   and washed

Roast chilli sauce
8 medium red chillies
50 g (1^3/$_4$ oz) palm sugar, grated
1 tablespoon fish sauce
1–2 tablespoons lime juice

Serves 6

To make the roast chilli sauce, roast the whole chillies over a naked flame or under a hot grill (broiler) until the skins blister and begin to blacken. Allow the chillies to cool, then remove the skins and scrape out the seeds. Using a mortar and pestle, pound the chillies with the palm sugar. Add the fish sauce and lime juice, to taste — the sauce should be a balance of hot, sweet and sour.

Cut the tentacles off the squid and reserve. Cut out the sharp beak and rinse the squid. Peel and discard the outer skin and membrane, then rinse again. Pat the squid dry and slice it in half lengthwise. Using a very sharp knife, score the underside of the flesh in a diamond pattern.

Generously season the flour with sea salt and freshly ground black pepper. Heat the oil in a deep-fat fryer or large saucepan to 180°C (350°F), or until a piece of bread fries golden brown in 15 seconds when dropped into the oil. Toss the squid and tentacles liberally in the flour, then shake off the excess. Deep-fry the squid in batches until golden. Drain on paper towels.

To serve, arrange the fried squid and tentacles in the centre of each serving plate. Spoon the roast chilli sauce over and around the squid. Top with the coriander sprigs.

to drink
Richmond Grove Silver Series Riesling, Barossa Valley, South Australia
The rich floral grapefruit aromatics tame and complement the spicy heat of roasted chillies.

shaved artichokes and parmesan

Great food is simply about texture and flavour, but to achieve this, the quality of the raw product must be paramount. Using Parmigiano Reggiano and the best extra virgin olive oil you can afford really makes this dish.

5 lemons
9 medium globe artichokes
extra virgin olive oil
a handful of flat-leaf (Italian) parsley, leaves picked,
    washed and roughly chopped
sea salt
100 g (3$^1/_2$ oz/1 cup) shaved Parmigiano Reggiano
warm crusty Italian-style bread, to serve

Serves 6

Add the juice of three of the lemons to a bowl of water. Working with one artichoke at a time, carefully pull away the tough, dark-green outer leaves and cut off the tips. Using a peeler or paring knife, peel or shave the outer layer of fibres from the stem and base of the choke. Use a teaspoon to scoop out the furry choke, if necessary (most modern varieties do not have one). Immediately put the artichokes in the acidulated water as they will discolour quickly once cut.

Drain the artichokes well and pat dry with paper towels. Cut in half and then, using a sharp knife or mandolin, shave lengthwise into very thin slices.

Put the shaved artichokes in a bowl with the juice of the remaining lemons, a good splash of olive oil, parsley, sea salt and freshly ground black pepper. Toss to mix.

To serve, divide the shaved artichokes among the serving plates and scatter with the Parmigiano Reggiano. Serve with warm crusty bread.

to drink
Primo Estate Joseph d'Elena Pinot Grigio, South Australia
The combination of rich, uniquely-flavoured artichoke and sharp Parmesan was made for the robust, savoury structure of food-friendly, Italian white varietals.

asparagus with champagne and saffron vinaigrette

30 asparagus spears, trimmed
200 g (7 oz) English spinach leaves, shredded
1/2 red capsicum (pepper), finely diced
1/2 yellow capsicum (pepper), finely diced

Champagne and saffron vinaigrette
a pinch of saffron threads (about 10 threads)
60 ml (2 fl oz/1/4 cup) champagne vinegar or
    best-quality white wine vinegar
1 teaspoon Dijon mustard
125 ml (4 fl oz/1/2 cup) extra virgin olive oil
a pinch of sugar

Serves 6

Blanch the asparagus spears briefly in boiling salted water, then refresh in iced water, drain and set aside.

To make the champagne and saffron vinaigrette, gently heat the saffron threads in a frying pan. Remove from the heat and add 2 tablespoons water. Transfer the saffron mixture to a bowl and whisk in the vinegar and mustard. Continue to whisk while adding the oil. Season with salt, freshly ground black pepper and the sugar.

To serve, place the shredded spinach in the centre of each serving plate. Top with the asparagus spears, drizzle with the vinaigrette, then scatter with the diced capsicum.

note
Purchasing champagne or wine vinegars is no different to buying quality wine; buy the best you can afford and you won't be disappointed. (Believe me, the difference between good and bad vinegars is huge!)

to drink
Andrew Harris Mudgee Verdelho, New South Wales
Verdelho is a great choice for this dish, as the flavours of tropical passionfruit and lime allow the delicate champagne and saffron to shine through.

tomato and porcini mushroom soup with parmesan crostini

75 g (2¹/₂ oz) dried porcini mushrooms
500 g (1 lb 2 oz/¹/₂ bunch) celery, outer
    stalks removed
olive oil
2 red onions, sliced
2 carrots, peeled and diced
2 tablespoons picked, washed and chopped
    thyme leaves
4 garlic cloves, thinly sliced

2 x 800 g (1 lb 12 oz) tins peeled, diced Roma
    (plum) tomatoes
70 g (2¹/₂ oz/¹/₂ bunch) flat-leaf (Italian) parsley, leaves
    picked, washed and roughly chopped

Parmesan crostini
1 loaf ciabatta, sliced
100 g (3¹/₂ oz/1 cup) grated Parmesan cheese

Serves 6

Soak the porcini mushrooms in 500 ml (17 fl oz/2 cups) boiling water for 15 minutes.

Slice the celery heart and green leaves. Heat a little oil in a large saucepan and gently sauté the onion, carrot and celery until tender and lightly coloured. Add the thyme and garlic and season with salt and freshly ground black pepper. Cook for 2 minutes to infuse the flavours.

Drain the porcini mushrooms and reserve the soaking liquid, leaving behind any sediment. Coarsely chop the porcini if they are large. Add the porcini mushrooms to the saucepan and sauté for a few minutes. Add the tomato and cook for 30–45 minutes, or until the tomato begins to thicken. Stir in the reserved porcini liquid and 1 litre (35 fl oz/4 cups) water. Simmer for a further 30 minutes, or until the soup has thickened. Add the parsley, check the seasoning and cook for a further 2 minutes.

To make the Parmesan crostini, toast the ciabatta slices. Sprinkle each slice with Parmesan and cook under a medium grill (broiler) until the cheese has melted.

To serve, ladle the soup into six serving bowls and serve with the Parmesan crostini.

to drink
Penfolds Rawson's Retreat Merlot, Barossa Valley, South Australia
A steaming bowl of hearty soup plus the wine's plum and dark chocolate flavours — the only other requirement on a rainy winter's day is an open log fire.

salmon with sorrel beurre blanc

This dish was made famous by brothers Jean and Pierre Troisgros at their restaurant in Roanne, near Lyon, France. To me, it has an elegant simplicity that is timeless.

extra virgin olive oil
700 g (1 lb 9 oz) salmon, skinned and pin-boned
    (see glossary)
40 g (1^1/$_2$ oz/1 bunch) sorrel, leaves picked, washed
    and cut into strips

Beurre blanc
125 ml (4 fl oz/^{1}/$_2$ cup) white wine vinegar
125 ml (4 fl oz/^{1}/$_2$ cup) white wine
2 French shallots, thinly sliced
3 white peppercorns
1 bay leaf
250 ml (9 fl oz/1 cup) cream
150 g (5^1/$_2$ oz) unsalted butter, cubed
juice of ^{1}/$_2$ lemon
sea salt and freshly ground white pepper

Serves 6

Rub a little olive oil on the base of six heatproof serving plates. Slice the salmon very thinly and arrange on the plates in a circle in a thin even layer. Season with a good pinch of salt.

To make the beurre blanc, combine the vinegar, wine, shallots, peppercorns and bay leaf in a small saucepan over medium heat. Bring to the boil and cook until the liquid has reduced by two-thirds. Strain into a clean saucepan, return to the heat and whisk in the cream. Return to the boil and cook until the liquid has reduced by one-third. Briskly whisk in the butter, one piece at a time. The sauce should appear thick and glossy. Adjust to taste with the lemon juice and season with sea salt and freshly ground white pepper. Keep the sauce warm, but not on a direct heat — a thermos is ideal.

To serve, place the serving plates with the salmon under a hot grill (broiler) for 2–3 minutes, or until the salmon is opaque. Spoon the beurre blanc over the salmon, then scatter with the sorrel. Season with freshly ground black pepper.

to drink
Mount Pleasant 'Lovedale' Semillon, Hunter Valley, New South Wales
Semillon from Australia's Hunter Valley is world renowned. Its toasty honey and grapefruit flavours work wonderfully with salmon, or just enjoy a glass for the sheer pleasure of it.

salt cod brandade with rocket and crostini

500 g (1 lb 2 oz) salt cod
1 litre (35 fl oz/4 cups) milk
several cloves
1 bay leaf
1 small onion, peeled
a few parsley sprigs, leaves picked and washed
250 g (9 oz) potatoes, peeled
125 ml (4 fl oz/1/2 cup) extra virgin olive oil
1 garlic clove, finely chopped
a pinch of freshly grated nutmeg

2 pinches of cayenne pepper
freshly ground white pepper
1 tablespoon lemon juice
2 large handfuls of rocket (arugula), stems
   removed, washed

Crostini
1 baguette, sliced
extra virgin olive oil

Serves 6

Soak the salt cod in cold water for 24 hours, changing the water several times.

Put the cod in a large saucepan with enough milk to cover the cod. Use several cloves to stick the bay leaf to the onion. Add the onion and parsley sprigs to the saucepan. Bring to the boil, then reduce the heat and gently simmer for several minutes, or until the cod is tender. Remove the saucepan from the heat and set aside for 15–20 minutes, or until the cod is cool.

Remove the cod from the milk. Strain and reserve the milk. Remove any skin and bones from the cod and flake the flesh into a bowl.

Cook the potato in a saucepan of boiling water until tender, then drain. Gently warm the olive oil in a small saucepan. Mash the potato with the garlic and briskly beat in the cod. Continue to beat, adding some of the warm milk, then some of the warm olive oil, alternating until you have a smooth mousse-like texture. Season with nutmeg, cayenne pepper and freshly ground white pepper. Adjust to taste with lemon juice.

To make the crostini, lightly drizzle the baguette slices with extra virgin olive oil and toast both sides under a hot grill (broiler).

To serve, scatter the rocket over each serving plate and spoon the brandade on top or alongside. Drizzle with a little extra virgin olive oil and a good grind of black pepper. Serve with the crostini.

to drink
Amberley Estate Chenin Blanc, Margaret River, Western Australia
Zesty apple and lychee leave the palate refreshingly clean — ready for another bite of crostini.

potato rösti, smoked salmon, watercress and crème fraîche

Potato rösti
3 large pink-skinned waxy potatoes, such as desiree,
    peeled (about 750 g/1 lb 10 oz)
1 teaspoon salt
100 g (3¹/₂ oz) clarified butter, melted (see essentials)

40 g (1¹/₂ oz) watercress, stems removed, washed
extra virgin olive oil
lemon juice
12 slices smoked salmon
60 ml (2 fl oz/¹/₄ cup) crème fraîche
50 g (1³/₄ oz) salmon caviar (optional)

Serves 6

To make the potato rösti, grate or slice the potatoes into thin batons on a mandolin. Sprinkle with the salt and set aside for 10 minutes. Squeeze out as much moisture as possible from the potato. Put the potato in a bowl and season with freshly ground black pepper.

Grease six egg rings with plenty of clarified butter and put in a frying pan over medium heat. Pack the potato mixture into the egg rings and cook until golden on one side. Brush liberally with clarified butter, turn over and cook the other side, turning again if necessary to ensure they are cooked through. Remove from the pan and keep warm. Repeat to make 6 rösti.

To serve, place one rösti in the centre of each serving plate. Dress the watercress lightly with a drizzle of olive oil and lemon juice and arrange on top of the rösti. Top with two slices of smoked salmon. Place a spoonful of crème fraîche on top and finish with a good grind of black pepper. Spoon the salmon caviar over the crème fraîche, if using.

to drink
Primo Estate Colombard, South Australia
It's hard to go wrong here — any crisp, herbaceous dry white wine will be delightful with the smoked salmon and crème fraîche.

sourdough toast with baked tomatoes, feta and basil

400 g (14 oz/2 punnets) cherry tomatoes or 6 small
   bunches vine-ripened tomatoes
extra virgin olive oil
6 slices sourdough
100 g (3^1/$_2$ oz) feta cheese, crumbled
a handful of basil, leaves picked and washed

Serves 6

Preheat the oven to 180°C (350°F/Gas 4) or a grill (broiler) to hot. Put the tomatoes on a large baking tray, drizzle with olive oil and season with salt and freshly ground black pepper. Bake or grill (broil) the tomatoes for 5–8 minutes, or until the skins have just split.

To serve, toast the sourdough and place a slice in the centre of each serving plate. Divide the cooked tomatoes among the sourdough slices and top with the crumbled feta and basil leaves. Finish with a good grind of black pepper and a drizzle of extra virgin olive oil.

to drink
Virgin Mary
Fresh tomato juice with a squeeze of lemon and lime makes for a great mid-morning pick-me-up. To make, pour tomato juice over ice in a tall glass, add a squeeze of lemon and lime juice, a dash of Worcestershire sauce, 2 or 3 drops of Tabasco sauce (to taste) and some salt and freshly ground black pepper. Serve with a celery stalk.

crab and spring onion omelette with chilli and palm sugar

500 g (1 lb 2 oz) cooked crab meat
4 spring onions (scallions), sliced
18 eggs
olive oil
butter

Chilli and palm sugar sauce
5 large red chillies
150 g (5 1/2 oz) palm sugar, grated
juice of 4 limes
2 tablespoons fish sauce

Serves 6

To make the chilli and palm sugar sauce, roast the whole chillies under a hot grill (broiler) until the skins begin to blister. Peel and discard the skins. Slice the chillies in half, scrape out the seeds and purée the chillies in a food processor. Dissolve the palm sugar in 1 tablespoon water mixed with the lime juice. Combine the palm sugar mixture, chilli purée and fish sauce. Add a little extra lime juice and fish sauce, to taste, if necessary.

Combine the crab meat with the spring onion, salt and freshly ground black pepper.

Preheat the oven to 120°C (240°F/Gas 1/2–1). Whisk three eggs with salt and freshly ground black pepper. Add a splash of olive oil and a small knob of butter to a 20 cm (8 inch) non-stick frying pan. Put over medium heat and, once the butter just starts to foam, pour the egg into the pan, gently moving the pan to spread the mixture evenly.

Leave for a few seconds until bubbles start to appear around the edge. Using a spatula or wooden spoon, gently break up the eggs so that the uncooked egg can fill the space, ensuring the eggs cook evenly. Cook until the egg is just set.

To serve, remove the pan from the heat and quickly place some of the crab mixture on the omelette. Fold the omelette in half and transfer to a baking tray. Place in the oven to keep warm. Repeat to make six omelettes.

When all are ready, transfer the omelettes to serving plates. Drizzle the chilli and palm sugar sauce over and around the omelettes and serve immediately.

to drink
d'Arenberg 'the Hermit Crab' Marsanne Viognier, McLaren Vale, South Australia
The sweet and sour flavours of this dish highlight the honeysuckle and white stone fruit characters of this luscious white Rhône-style blend.

baked parmesan and thyme tart with red onion jam

Shortcrust pastry
250 g (9 oz/2 cups) plain (all-purpose) flour
155 g (5^{1}/$_{2}$ oz) unsalted butter
a pinch of sea salt
80 ml (2^{1}/$_{2}$ fl oz/^{1}/$_{3}$ cup) chilled water
1 egg, beaten

Red onion jam
5 red onions
1 tablespoon olive oil
1 tablespoon unsalted butter
60 ml (2 fl oz/^{1}/$_{4}$ cup) red wine vinegar
1^{1}/$_{2}$ tablespoons soft brown sugar

Filling
1 tablespoon unsalted butter
1 onion, finely diced
300 ml (10^{1}/$_{2}$ fl oz/1^{1}/$_{4}$ cups) cream
3 eggs
150 g (5^{1}/$_{2}$ oz/1^{1}/$_{2}$ cups) grated Parmesan cheese
2 teaspoons picked, washed and chopped
   thyme leaves

shaved Parmesan cheese, to serve

Serves 6

To make the shortcrust pastry, process the flour, butter and salt in a food processor until the mixture resembles fine breadcrumbs. Add enough chilled water to bring the pastry together, but do not overwork it. Knead lightly, wrap in plastic wrap and refrigerate for 1 hour. Preheat the oven to 180°C (350°F/Gas 4). Roll out the pastry to a thickness of 3 mm (^{1}/$_{8}$ inch) and gently ease it into a 24 cm (9^{1}/$_{2}$ inch) tart tin. Refrigerate or freeze the pastry shell for 30 minutes.

Line the pastry shell with a piece of baking paper and baking beads (or dried beans or rice). Blind bake the pastry for 20–30 minutes, or until it is partially cooked and golden. Remove the paper and beads and brush the pastry with the beaten egg. Reduce the oven to 160°C (315°F/Gas 2–3) and bake the pastry for a further 10 minutes, or until golden. Reduce the oven to 120°C (250°F/Gas ^{1}/$_{2}$).

To make the red onion jam, peel and halve the onions lengthwise and remove the ends. Slice the onions into thin semicircles. Heat the oil and butter in a wide, shallow frying pan over medium heat. Sauté the onion, without colouring, for 10 minutes, or until tender. Add the vinegar and sugar and cook for 15–20 minutes, or until the onion is dark in colour and jam-like in consistency. If necessary, add some water during cooking to prevent the mixture from burning. Season with salt and freshly ground black pepper. Set aside to cool.

To make the filling, heat the butter in a small frying pan. Sauté the onion, without colouring, until soft. Set aside to cool. Whisk together the cream and eggs, then fold in the Parmesan, thyme and sautéed onion. Season well. Pour the mixture into the pastry shell and bake for 40–50 minutes, or until the filling is just set. To serve, place a wedge of warm tart in the centre of each plate. Scatter Parmesan over the tart and serve with red onion jam.

to drink
Yalumba 'Christobel's' Dry White, Barossa Valley, South Australia
Fragrant fruit and a lively sherbet palate marry well with the tart's rich egg-and-herb flavours.

fig, shallot and blue cheese tarts with rocket and hazelnuts

The key to this dish is balance. Try to choose a blue cheese that isn't too strong, as heating it can sometimes make the cheese appear stronger, which may affect the delicate flavour of the figs.

6 x 12 cm (5 inch) circles puff pastry (you will need about 2 sheets of pastry)
6 firm ripe figs, quartered
60 g (2¼ oz) blue cheese, crumbled
70 g (2½ oz/½ cup) hazelnuts, roasted and skins removed, roughly chopped
a large handful of rocket (arugula), stems removed, washed
extra virgin olive oil
balsamic vinegar or vincotto (see note)

Shallot jam
1 tablespoon olive oil
1 tablespoon unsalted butter
10 French shallots, sliced (about 300 g/10½ oz)
1 tablespoon red wine vinegar
50 g (1¾ oz/¼ cup) soft brown sugar
60 ml (2 fl oz/¼ cup) port
a few thyme sprigs, leaves picked and washed

Serves 6

To make the shallot jam, heat the olive oil and butter in a frying pan over medium heat. Add the shallots and sauté, without colouring, for 10 minutes, or until tender. Add the red wine vinegar and sugar and stir to dissolve. Cook for 15–20 minutes, or until the shallots are dark in colour and jam-like in consistency. Stir through the port and thyme and cook for several minutes. Remove the pan from the heat and allow to cool.

Preheat the oven to 220°C (425°F/Gas 7). Put the pastry circles on baking trays lined with baking paper. Prick the pastry circles with a fork and cover with the shallot jam. Arrange four fig quarters on each circle and scatter over the blue cheese. Bake for 15–20 minutes, or until the pastry is cooked and the tops begin to colour.

To serve, place each tart in the centre of a serving plate and scatter over the hazelnuts and rocket. Finish with a drizzle of extra virgin olive oil, a few drops of balsamic vinegar or vincotto and a grind of black pepper.

note
Vincotto is a grape syrup made by cooking the pulped grapes, or musts, of two grape varieties, which is then reduced in volume by one-fifth. The syrup is left to age in oak barrels for up to 4 years, developing quite a unique sweet and sour flavour.

to drink
Seresin Estate Pinot Gris, Marlborough, New Zealand
This pinot gris has full-bodied tropical fruit and pear flavours, with a slightly creamy texture — perfect for balancing the sharpness of the blue cheese.

grilled polenta with gorgonzola and oregano

1 litre (35 fl oz/4 cups) milk
1/2 onion
a few thyme sprigs, leaves picked and washed
1 rosemary sprig, leaves picked and washed
2 bay leaves
4 garlic cloves, halved
140 g (5 oz) polenta
60 g (2^1/4 oz/^{2}/3 cup) grated Parmesan cheese
1 tablespoon unsalted butter

115 g (4 oz) Gorgonzola cheese, thickly sliced
a small handful of oregano, leaves picked and washed

Serves 6

To make the polenta, put the milk, onion, herbs and garlic in a saucepan and heat until almost boiling. Put the polenta in a large saucepan. Strain the milk onto the polenta and whisk until blended.

Stir the polenta constantly over medium heat until boiling. Reduce the heat to very low and cook, stirring often, for 20–30 minutes, or until the polenta is very smooth and begins to thicken. Fold in the Parmesan and butter and season to taste with salt and freshly ground black pepper.

Grease a shallow 18 x 28 cm (7 x 11 inch) cake tin. Gently press the polenta into the tin and refrigerate for several hours.

Preheat the oven to 180°C (350°F/Gas 4). Cut the polenta into triangular wedges, about 10 cm (4 inches) in length, and transfer to a non-stick baking tray. Warm the polenta in the oven for 5 minutes. Put a slice of Gorgonzola on the thick part of each polenta wedge. Cook under a hot grill (broiler) until the Gorgonzola has just melted.

To serve, place the grilled polenta wedges on serving plates and scatter the oregano over the top.

to drink
Moondah Brook Verdelho, Western Australia
The sharp, tangy Gorgonzola mellows beautifully under the influence of the verdelho's rich, spicy, full flavours.

grilled quail with risotto bianco, grapes and verjuice

6 boned and butterflied quails (see glossary)
olive oil
a handful of small basil leaves, picked
   and washed
140 g (5 oz/³/4 cup) small seedless grapes
extra virgin olive oil
verjuice
sea salt and freshly ground white pepper

Risotto bianco
2 tablespoons olive oil
85 g (3 oz) unsalted butter
1 leek, white part only, diced
4 French shallots, sliced
2 garlic cloves, sliced
450 g (1 lb/2 cups) risotto rice
375 ml (13 fl oz/1¹/2 cups) white wine
1.5 litres (52 fl oz/6 cups) boiling chicken stock
70 g (2¹/2 oz/³/4 cup) grated Parmesan cheese
juice of ¹/2–1 lemon

Serves 6

To make the risotto bianco, heat the olive oil and half the butter in a saucepan over medium heat. Gently sauté the leek, shallots and garlic, without colouring, until tender. Add the rice and stir until it is well coated with oil.

Reduce the heat to low and stir in the wine. Cook until the wine is almost completely absorbed by the rice. Stir in 250 ml (9 fl oz/1 cup) of the boiling stock and cook until the stock is almost absorbed. Continue adding stock and cooking in this way, stirring frequently, until the stock is absorbed and the rice is al dente.

Meanwhile, preheat the oven to 200°C (400°F/Gas 6). Heat an ovenproof frying pan over high heat. Brush the quails with olive oil, season with salt and freshly ground black pepper and sear, skin side down, until golden brown. Turn the quails over and transfer the pan to the oven. Bake for 4–5 minutes, or until cooked through. Set aside to rest briefly.

Fold the Parmesan and remaining butter through the risotto. Season with salt and freshly ground black pepper and adjust to taste with lemon juice.

Combine the basil with the grapes, a good splash of extra virgin olive oil, a splash of verjuice and a good grind of black pepper. To serve, divide the risotto among serving bowls, place the quail on top and spoon over the grape mixture.

to drink
Seresin Estate 'Marama' Sauvignon blanc, Marlborough, New Zealand
This barrel-fermented white Bordeaux style comes into its own when paired with quail and sweet fresh grapes.

shaved pear and fennel salad with goat's curd

This salad has what I consider a near-perfect balance of flavours — the crisp pear and fennel marrying beautifully with the goat's curd and honey.

2 medium fennel bulbs, very thinly sliced
a small handful of flat-leaf (Italian) parsley, leaves
   picked, washed and roughly chopped
1/2 small red onion, thinly sliced
6 firm pears, thinly sliced lengthwise, cores intact
   (see note)
240 g (8 1/2 oz) goat's curd
good-quality honey (see note)

Lemon and Dijon mustard dressing
2 teaspoons lemon juice
2 tablespoons extra virgin olive oil
1/2 teaspoon wholegrain mustard
2 teaspoons Dijon mustard
1 teaspoon good-quality honey
sea salt

Serves 6

To make the lemon and Dijon mustard dressing, whisk the lemon juice, olive oil, mustards and honey until well combined. Season to taste with sea salt and freshly ground black pepper.

Combine the sliced fennel, parsley and red onion in a bowl. Moisten with the lemon and Dijon mustard dressing.

To serve, place a slice of pear in the centre of each serving plate. Top with a small pile of salad, then another pear slice. Continue layering the salad and pear slices. Place small spoonfuls of goat's curd on top and around the salad. Drizzle lightly with honey and finish with a good grind of black pepper.

note
A mandolin is ideal for slicing the pears, but watch your fingers!
With regards to the choice of honey, I prefer one that is not too sweet, such as New Zealand Manuka honey, but there are many wonderful varieties out there, just use one you like.

to drink
St. Hallets Poachers Blend, Barossa Valley, South Australia
This crisp, clean, easy drinking blend of chenin blanc, semillon and sauvignon blanc allows the delicate flavours of pear and fennel to show through.

I firmly believe that you must start with great produce

but learning good techniques is equally as important.

seared scallops, chorizo, celeriac purée and petite salade

olive oil
3 chorizo sausages, sliced
36 scallops
extra virgin olive oil, to serve

Celeriac purée
1 large or 2 small celeriac, peeled and diced
4 garlic cloves, peeled
2 bay leaves
600 ml (20 fl oz/2^1/2 cups) milk
1 tablespoon unsalted butter

Petite salade
100 g (3^1/2 oz) mixed salad leaves, such as watercress,
　　frisée and rocket (arugula), picked and washed
extra virgin olive oil
juice of 1 lemon

Serves 6

To make the celeriac purée, put the celeriac, garlic and bay leaves in a saucepan. Add enough milk to cover. Bring to the boil, then reduce the heat and simmer for 15–20 minutes, or until tender. Strain the celeriac, discarding the garlic and bay leaves and reserving the milk. Transfer to a food processor and process until smooth. Add the butter and enough of the reserved milk to form a smooth purée. Season with salt and freshly ground black pepper. Set aside and keep warm.

Heat a little olive oil in a frying pan over medium to high heat. Fry the chorizo slices on both sides. Remove from the pan and keep warm.

Rinse the pan and return to high heat. Season the scallops with a little olive oil, salt and freshly ground black pepper. Quickly sear the scallops on both sides, in batches, until just cooked and still moist.

To make the petite salade, add the extra virgin olive oil and lemon juice to the salad leaves to moisten. To serve, place a spoonful of the celeriac purée in the centre of each serving plate. Arrange the scallops and chorizo on top. Drizzle with a little extra virgin olive oil and serve with the salad on top.

note
The celeriac purée can be prepared ahead and refrigerated. Warm it in a small saucepan over low heat when ready to serve.

to drink
Pierro LTC Semillon Sauvignon Blanc, Margaret River, Western Australia
A little touch of chardonnay in this refreshing blend provides the weight needed to balance the spicy chorizo.

salad of green mango, prawns, chilli, lime and cashews

Crisp, tart green mangoes give this salad vitality. Adjust the dressing to your palate by using the Thai principle of sweet, sour and salty — if it's too sweet, add a little extra lime juice, if it's too sharp, add palm sugar and if salt is required, add a dash of fish sauce.

oil, for cooking
20 g (^{3}/4 oz/^{1}/4 cup) julienned fresh ginger
500 g (1 lb 2 oz) cooked, peeled and deveined
   prawns (shrimp), with tails intact
85 g (3 oz/^{1}/2 cup) roasted unsalted cashews

Palm sugar and lime dressing
150 ml (5 fl oz) lime juice
150 g (5^1/2 oz) palm sugar, finely chopped
1 kaffir lime (makrut) leaf
1 lemongrass stalk, white part only, roughly chopped
a small handful of coriander roots, roughly chopped
   (about ^{1}/4 cup)
1–2 tablespoons fish sauce

Salad
2 green mangoes, skin removed, cut into thin strips
1 medium red chilli, seeded and thinly sliced
3 French shallots, thinly sliced
2 spring onions (scallions), thinly sliced on
   the diagonal
a large handful of coriander (cilantro), leaves picked
   and washed
a handful of Thai basil, leaves picked and washed
60 g (2^1/4 oz) baby English spinach, stems
   removed, washed

Serves 6

To make the palm sugar and lime dressing, put the lime juice in a saucepan over medium heat and bring it to the boil. Remove from the heat, add the palm sugar and stir until it has dissolved. Using a mortar and pestle, crush the lime leaf, lemongrass and coriander roots. Add the lime leaf mixture to the lime juice mixture, then add the fish sauce, to taste. Set aside for 1 hour for the flavours to infuse. Strain and refrigerate the dressing until required.

To make the salad, combine the ingredients in a bowl. Add enough of the palm sugar and lime dressing to moisten the salad.

Heat some oil in a saucepan over medium heat. Fry the ginger until crisp, then drain on paper towels.

To serve, toss the prawns wth the salad and divide among six serving plates. Scatter the cashews over the top and drizzle with extra dressing. Top with the fried ginger.

to drink
Sandalford Chenin Verdelho, Western Australia
With a crisp, herbaceous glass of wine in one hand and a plate of prawn and mango salad in the other, you could almost be on the balmy beach of your dreams.

smoked quail with watercress, apple and hazelnuts

6 smoked quails (see note)
honey, extra

Dijon mustard and honey dressing
80 ml (2^1/$_2$ fl oz/^{1}/$_3$ cup) fresh orange juice
2 teaspoons Dijon mustard
80 ml (2^1/$_2$ fl oz/^{1}/$_3$ cup) hazelnut oil or extra virgin
    olive oil
2 tablespoons honey

Salad
3 fuji or red apples, unpeeled, thinly sliced
a small handful of flat-leaf (Italian) parsley, leaves
    picked and washed
1 red witlof (chicory/Belgian endive), leaves separated
1 green witlof (chicory/Belgian endive), leaves
    separated
1 large handful of rocket (arugula), stems
    removed, washed
40 g (1^1/$_2$ oz/1 bunch) watercress, stems
    removed, washed
^{1}/$_2$ red onion, thinly sliced
100 g (3^1/$_2$ oz/^{3}/$_4$ cup) roasted hazelnuts, skinned and
    roughly chopped

Serves 6

To make the Dijon mustard and honey dressing, whisk the orange juice, mustard, oil and honey until combined.

Preheat the oven to 200°C (400°F/Gas 6). Quarter each quail to give two breast and two leg pieces. Put the quail pieces on a baking tray, lightly brush with a little honey and warm in the oven for 2–3 minutes until heated through.

To make the salad, combine the ingredients in a bowl. Add enough of the Dijon mustard and honey dressing to moisten the salad. To serve, arrange half the salad on serving plates. Add two quail breasts to each plate, then top with the remaining salad and quail legs. Spoon over extra dressing if required.

note
Smoked quail are available from good delicatessens. If they are unavailable, use smoked chicken or grilled (broiled) fresh quail.

to drink
Tamar Ridge 'Devil's Corner' Pinot Noir, Tasmania
Delicate smoked quail and the spicy plums and cherries of a great pinot noir — a classic combination.

hazelnut-crumbed lamb brains and celeriac remoulade

9 lamb brains, soaked overnight in salted water

1 carrot, peeled and roughly chopped

1 leek, white part only, roughly chopped

1 celery stalk, roughly chopped

1 onion, roughly chopped

2 bay leaves

sea salt

6 black peppercorns

a splash of white vinegar

125 ml (4 fl oz/^{1}/$_2$ cup) milk

1 egg

60 g (2^1/$_4$ oz/^{1}/$_2$ cup) plain (all-purpose) flour

160 g (5^3/$_4$ oz/2 cups) fresh breadcrumbs

70 g (2^1/$_2$ oz/^{1}/$_2$ cup) hazelnuts, roasted, skins
   removed and chopped

olive oil, for cooking

Celeriac remoulade

^{1}/$_2$ small celeriac, julienned

4 anchovies, finely chopped

1 tablespoon capers, rinsed

40 g (1^1/$_2$ oz/^{1}/$_3$ cup) gherkins, finely chopped

a handful of flat-leaf (Italian) parsley, leaves picked,
   washed and finely chopped

^{1}/$_4$ teaspoon grated lemon zest

125 g (4^1/$_2$ oz/^{1}/$_2$ cup) good-quality mayonnaise

Petite salade

100 g (3^1/$_2$ oz) mixed salad leaves, picked
   and washed

lemon juice

extra virgin olive oil or hazelnut oil

Serves 6

Drain the lamb brains and put them in a saucepan. Cover with fresh water and add the carrot, leek, celery, onion, bay leaves, sea salt, black peppercorns and a splash of vinegar. Cook over very low heat until the liquid is almost boiling, but do not allow it to boil. Remove from the heat and set aside until the brains are cool. Remove the brains and carefully cut in half, discarding any connective tissue.

Whisk together the milk and egg and season with salt and ground black pepper. Toss the brains in the flour, shaking off the excess. Dip into the egg mixture, then coat with the combined breadcrumbs and hazelnuts.

To make the celeriac remoulade, combine the celeriac, anchovies, capers, gherkins, parsley and lemon zest. Add enough mayonnaise to moisten the ingredients. Season to taste with salt and ground black pepper.

To make the petite salade, moisten the salad leaves with the lemon juice and extra virgin olive oil or hazelnut oil.

Heat some olive oil in a shallow frying pan over medium heat. Fry the brains in batches, turning regularly, until crisp and golden. Drain on paper towels.

To serve, arrange three brain halves on each serving plate. Place a spoonful of celeriac remoulade and a small handful of petite salade to the side.

to drink
Stoniers Reserve Pinot Noir, Mornington Peninsula, Victoria
Light-bodied red wines such as pinot noir combine well with the unique texture of this dish.

roast chicken with red onion, penne, olives, rocket and garlic

1 bulb of garlic, roughly chopped
a few thyme sprigs, leaves picked and washed
1 lemon, roughly chopped
1.6 kg (3 lb 8 oz) chicken
extra virgin olive oil
3 red onions
balsamic vinegar

500 g (1 lb 2 oz) penne
3 garlic cloves, extra, thinly sliced
100 g (3^1/$_2$ oz) rocket (arugula), stems
    removed, washed
90 g (3^1/$_4$ oz/^{1}/$_2$ cup) black olives
a pinch of chilli flakes

Serves 6–8

Preheat the oven to 200°C (400°F/Gas 6). Combine the garlic, thyme and lemon. Push the mixture into the cavity of the chicken. Rub the skin with extra virgin olive oil and season with salt and freshly ground black pepper. Put the chicken in a roasting tin and bake for 1–1^1/$_4$ hours, or until cooked through. Remove from the oven and set aside.

Reduce the oven to 180°C (350°F/Gas 4). Line a baking tray with baking paper. Peel and cut the onions into wedges, leaving the root end intact to hold the segments together. Put the onion wedges on the tray, drizzle with extra virgin olive oil and balsamic vinegar and season with salt and freshly ground black pepper. Bake for 15–20 minutes, or until tender.

Meanwhile, cook the penne in a large saucepan of boiling salted water for 8–10 minutes, or until al dente. Drain the penne.

Heat a little extra virgin olive oil in a frying pan over medium heat. Sauté the sliced garlic for 2–3 minutes, or until slightly coloured.

To serve, remove the meat from the chicken and combine with the onion, rocket, olives, chilli flakes, fried garlic and penne in a large bowl. Add a little extra virgin olive oil and season with salt and freshly ground black pepper. Arrange the salad in the centre of serving plates. Serve warm or at room temperature.

to drink
Temple Bruer Grenache Shiraz Viognier, Langhorne Creek, South Australia
For a Sunday lunch or light dinner with friends you can't beat this raspberry and wild blackberry dominant blend.

blue cheese fettuccine with spinach and pine nuts

Try this sauce with potato gnocchi — you can't go wrong either way.

2 tablespoons olive oil
100 g (3¹/2 oz) French shallots, sliced
3 garlic cloves, sliced
125 ml (4 fl oz/¹/2 cup) dry white wine
300 ml (10¹/2 fl oz/1¹/4 cups) cream
200 g (7 oz) baby English spinach, stems
    removed, washed

80 g (3 oz) Gorgonzola cheese, roughly chopped
juice of ¹/2 lemon
250 g (9 oz) fettuccine
shaved Parmesan cheese, to serve
40 g (1¹/2 oz/¹/4 cup) pine nuts, roasted, to serve

Serves 6

Heat the olive oil in a frying pan over medium heat. Sauté the shallots and garlic, without colouring, until tender. Pour in the wine and simmer until reduced by half, stirring, to deglaze the pan. Add the cream and simmer until the mixture has reduced by one-third. Add the spinach, Gorgonzola and lemon juice. Season to taste with salt and freshly ground black pepper.

Cook the fettuccine in a large saucepan of boiling salted water for 7–8 minutes, or until al dente. Drain the fettuccine and fold through the sauce. If the sauce appears too thick, add a little boiling water to thin it.

To serve, use a pair of tongs and a large spoon to divide the pasta among shallow serving bowls. Top with shaved Parmesan, scatter with the pine nuts and finish with a good grind of black pepper.

to drink
Craggy Range 'Rapaura Road' Riesling, Marlborough, New Zealand
Blue cheese and pine nuts provide the perfect counterbalance to the almost Germanic characteristics of this world class New Zealand riesling.

Restraint is paramount — one of the greatest

attributes a cook can have is to know when to stop.

potato and rosemary pizzas

Pizza base
1$^1/_2$ teaspoons dried yeast
150–175 ml (5$^1/_2$–6 fl oz) lukewarm water
225 g (8 oz/1$^3/_4$ cups) bread flour
a pinch of sugar
2 tablespoons extra virgin olive oil
$^1/_2$ teaspoon salt

2–3 medium potatoes
sea salt
100 g (3$^1/_2$ oz/1 cup) shaved Parmesan cheese
extra virgin olive oil
2 rosemary sprigs, leaves picked, washed
  and chopped
truffle oil, to serve

Serves 4

To make the pizza base, combine the yeast with 60 ml (2 fl oz/$^1/_4$ cup) of the lukewarm water, 30 g (1 oz/ $^1/_4$ cup) of the flour and the sugar in the bowl of an electric mixer. Set aside for 30 minutes. After this time, the yeast will have activated and be frothy.

Add the oil, salt and remaining flour to the yeast mixture and knead with a dough hook. (Alternatively, knead by hand for 5–8 minutes.) Add enough of the remaining lukewarm water to make a tacky dough. Knead until the dough is smooth and elastic. Cover the bowl with plastic wrap and set aside in a warm place until the dough has doubled in size.

Turn the dough out onto a heavily floured surface, divide into quarters and roll each piece into a ball. Lightly oil a baking sheet or pizza tray. Using floured hands or a rolling pin, flatten the dough to form 15 cm (6 inch) circles. Put on the baking sheet or tray and set aside while preparing the topping.

Preheat the oven to 250°C (500°F/Gas 9). Wash the potatoes and slice them into very thin rounds. Sprinkle with sea salt and set aside for 10 minutes. Rinse the potato slices and pat dry.

Cover the pizza bases with some of the Parmesan. Arrange the potato slices over the top, lightly brush with extra virgin olive oil and bake for 10 minutes. Sprinkle with the rosemary and top with the remaining Parmesan. Bake for a further 7–10 minutes, or until the crust is cooked through.

To serve, drizzle the pizzas with truffle oil and finish with a grind of black pepper.

to drink
Coldstream Hills Reserve Merlot, Yarra Valley, Victoria
A casual get together with friends. What better excuse for home-made pizza and an elegant glass of red?

cuttlefish with garlic, basil, tomato and angel hair pasta

500 g (1 lb 2 oz) medium-sized cuttlefish
extra virgin olive oil
250 g (9 oz) angel hair pasta
a large handful of basil, leaves picked, washed
   and torn
extra virgin olive oil, to serve

Tomato sauce
2 tablespoons olive oil
4 garlic cloves, thinly sliced
2 cinnamon sticks, broken
250 ml (9 fl oz/1 cup) white wine
2 x 400 g (14 oz) tins whole peeled tomatoes,
   roughly chopped

Serves 6

To make the tomato sauce, heat the olive oil in a saucepan over medium heat. Sauté the garlic and cinnamon for 2–3 minutes, or until slightly coloured (do not allow it to colour too much or it may become bitter). Add the wine and cook for several minutes to reduce the sauce. Add the chopped tomatoes and juice and season with salt and freshly ground black pepper. Reduce the heat and simmer for 20 minutes. Set aside to cool, then remove the cinnamon pieces.

Slice the cuttlefish lengthwise through the body. Open the body and remove the insides, including the cuttle bone. Pull away the skin and membrane and discard it with the tentacles. Using a very sharp knife, score the underside of the flesh in a diamond pattern. Lightly toss the cuttlefish with extra virgin olive oil and refrigerate until required.

Cook the pasta in a large saucepan of boiling salted water for 8–10 minutes, or until al dente. Drain the pasta.

Meanwhile, heat a frying pan over high heat. Drain the excess oil from the cuttlefish and season with salt and freshly ground black pepper. Put the cuttlefish, scored side down, in the hot pan and cook until golden and cooked through, turning once. Remove the cuttlefish from the pan.

Return the pan to the heat and add the tomato sauce. Bring the sauce to a gentle simmer, then remove from the heat and fold through the basil and the pasta. Gently toss to combine. To serve, divide the pasta among serving bowls. Arrange the cuttlefish on top and finish with a drizzle of extra virgin olive oil and a good grind of black pepper.

to drink
Masi 'Bonacosta' Valpolicella Classico, Italy
Tomato, seafood, pasta; when in Italy, eat and drink with the locals.

meals to linger over

I would love to be able to tell you that all my recipes take 10–15 minutes to prepare, but sometimes a little extra effort is required. Just like life, you only get out of it what you put in but, believe me, it's worth it.

braised oxtail and potato soup with garlic ciabatta

Braised oxtail

plain (all-purpose) flour, for dusting

1.5 kg (3 lb 5 oz) oxtail pieces

olive oil

1 onion, roughly chopped

1 carrot, peeled and roughly chopped

1 celery stalk, roughly chopped

1 leek, white part only, halved lengthwise and chopped

5 garlic cloves, unpeeled, lightly crushed

a few rosemary sprigs, leaves picked and washed

a few thyme sprigs, leaves picked and washed

3 tablespoons tomato paste (purée)

400 ml (14 fl oz/1^1/2 cups) red wine

2 litres (70 fl oz/8 cups) beef stock

3 small bulbs of garlic, cloves separated, unpeeled

olive oil

2 tablespoons unsalted butter

1 large leek, white part only, sliced

1 large red onion, diced

2 celery stalks, diced

3 garlic cloves, sliced

350 g (12 oz) waxy potatoes, peeled and diced

2 tablespoons sherry

12 slices ciabatta

a handful of flat-leaf (Italian) parsley, leaves picked,
  washed and roughly chopped, to serve

Serves 6

To braise the oxtail, preheat the oven to 160°C (315°F/Gas 2–3). Season the flour with salt and freshly ground black pepper. Lightly coat the oxtail in the flour, then shake off the excess. Heat some olive oil in a frying pan. Seal the oxtail pieces well, transferring them to a large flameproof casserole as they brown. Add the onion, carrot, celery, leek, garlic and herbs to the frying pan and cook until golden. Add the tomato paste and cook for 5 minutes. Spoon the mixture over the oxtail in the casserole.

Deglaze the pan with the wine, stirring to loosen the sediment. Pour into the casserole. Add enough stock to the casserole to cover the oxtail and vegetables and bring to the boil. Transfer to the oven and bake, covered, for 2–2^1/2 hours, or until the meat pulls away from the bones. Set aside for the oxtail to cool in the stock.

Put the garlic on a sheet of aluminium foil, drizzle liberally with olive oil and fold up loosely. Bake on a baking tray for 30–40 minutes, or until the garlic is tender. Meanwhile, remove the oxtail meat from the bones, discarding any fat or sinew. Strain the stock, discarding the vegetables. You want 1.5–2 litres (52–70 fl oz/ 6–8 cups) of stock. Make up the quantity with water, if need be.

Heat the butter in a large saucepan over medium heat. Sauté the leek, onion, celery and garlic, without colouring, for 6–8 minutes, or until tender. Add the potato, season and cook for a further 5 minutes.

Pour in the strained stock and bring to the boil, skimming any impurities that rise to the surface. Reduce the heat and simmer until the potato is tender. Add the oxtail meat and return to the boil. Check the seasoning and stir through the sherry. Squeeze the garlic flesh into a bowl. Toast the ciabatta slices, then spread with the garlic. To serve, ladle the soup into serving bowls, sprinkle with the parsley and serve with the garlic ciabatta.

to drink

Taylor's Cabernet Sauvignon, Clare Valley, South Australia
Rich, hearty and soul warming — true of both the soup and this delicious Australian cabernet sauvignon.

Food has always been and always will be about flavour.

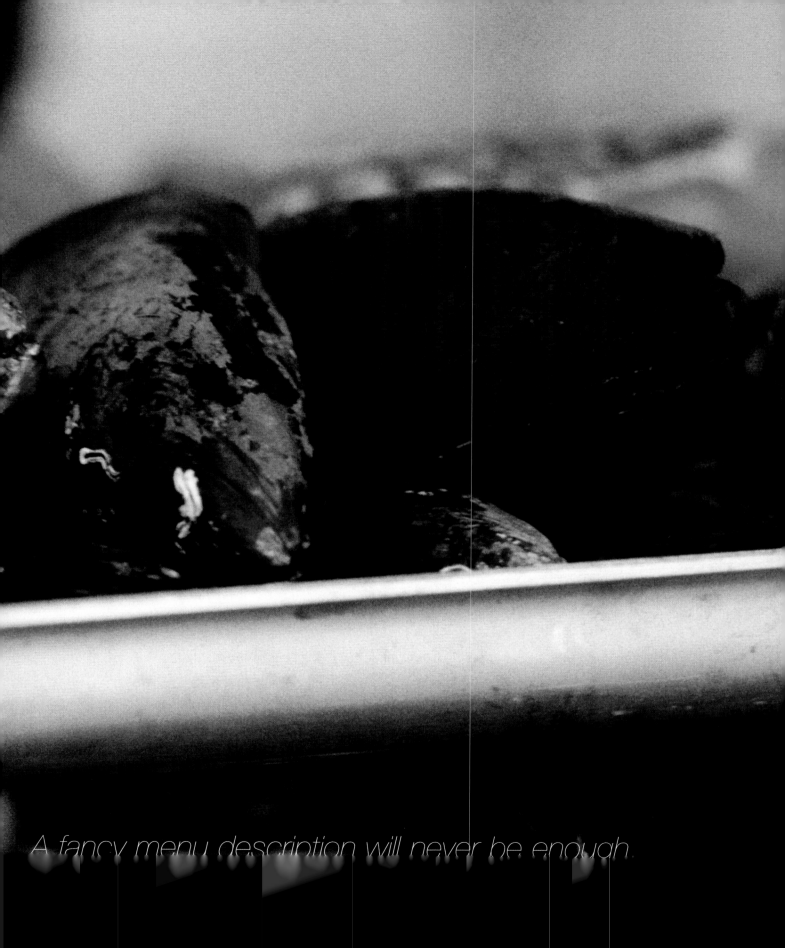

A fancy menu description will never be enough.

fisherman's soup

Soup base
olive oil
1 large red onion, diced
2 celery stalks, diced
1 baby fennel bulb, sliced, tips reserved
1 garlic clove, crushed
500 ml (17 fl oz/2 cups) white wine
2 x 400 g (14 oz) tins diced tomatoes
a pinch of saffron threads
chilli flakes, to taste

500 g (1 lb 2 oz) black mussels, cleaned, beards removed
olive oil
12 medium raw prawns (shrimp), peeled and deveined, tails intact
18 scallops (about 300 g/10^1/$_2$ oz)
225 g (8 oz) white fish, cubed
225 g (8 oz) salmon, cubed

Serves 6

To make the soup base, heat some olive oil in a large saucepan over medium heat. Sauté the onion, celery, sliced fennel bulb and garlic, without colouring, for 6–8 minutes, or until tender. Add the wine and bring to the boil, then reduce the heat and simmer until the wine has reduced by half.

Add the tomato, saffron and chilli flakes. Return to the boil and cook for 5 minutes, or until thickened slightly. Add 250 ml (9 fl oz/1 cup) hot water and gently simmer for 15 minutes. Season with salt and freshly ground black pepper. If the soup base is too thick, adjust the consistency with more water. Remove from the heat.

Discard any mussels that are broken or cracked or do not close when tapped.

Heat a little olive oil in a large saucepan over medium heat. Cook the prawns, scallops and mussels for several minutes, or until the prawns are opaque and the mussels have opened. Discard any mussels that do not open. Pour the hot soup base over the seafood, add the white fish and cook, covered, for 2–3 minutes, or until the fish is cooked through. Fold through the salmon.

To serve, divide the soup among serving bowls. Chop the reserved fennel tips and scatter over the soup.

to drink
Garry Crittenden 'I' Sangiovese, King Valley, Victoria
Northern Victoria's King Valley produces some wonderful Italian varietals. What could be better with this tomato-based soup?

twice-baked goat's cheese soufflé with apple and walnut salad

140 g (5 oz) unsalted butter

140 g (5 oz/heaped 1 cup) plain (all-purpose) flour

700 ml (24 fl oz/2^3/$_4$ cups) warm milk

250 g (9 oz) goat's cheese, mashed

2 tablespoons grated Parmesan cheese

1 tablespoon Dijon mustard

1 tablespoon picked, washed and chopped
   thyme leaves

6 eggs, separated

Parmesan glaze

125 ml (4 fl oz/^{1}/$_2$ cup) cream

60 g (^{2}/$_3$ cup/2^1/$_4$ oz) grated Parmesan cheese

2 egg yolks

Apple and walnut salad

a handful of frisée, leaves picked and washed

a handful of watercress or rocket (arugula), stems
   removed and washed

2 red apples, thinly sliced

1 tablespoon picked, washed and chopped
   chive leaves

50 g (1^3/$_4$ oz/^{1}/$_2$ cup) roasted walnuts, chopped

red wine vinegar

extra virgin olive oil

Serves 8

Preheat the oven to 180°C (350°F/Gas 4). Melt 1 tablespoon of the butter and grease eight 185 ml (6 fl oz/ ^{3}/$_4$ cup) capacity soufflé dishes. Melt the remaining butter in a large saucepan over medium heat. Add the flour and mix well. Cook over low heat for 5–8 minutes, stirring with a wooden spoon. Gradually whisk in the warm milk, a little at a time, stirring constantly to avoid any lumps forming. Continue until all the milk has been used, then reduce the heat to very low and cook for a further 5–8 minutes. Remove from the heat, adjust the seasoning, then strain. Set aside to cool slightly.

Stir the goat's cheese, Parmesan, mustard and thyme into the warm mixture. Set aside to cool. Beat the egg yolks into the cooled mixture and season with salt and freshly ground white pepper. In a clean, dry bowl, whisk the egg whites until they hold medium peaks. Use a metal spoon to fold the egg whites into the soufflé mixture.

Divide the mixture among the soufflé dishes and put the dishes in a roasting tin. Pour enough boiling water into the tin to reach halfway up the sides of the dishes. Bake the soufflés for 15–20 minutes, or until they are risen and evenly coloured. Remove the dishes from the tin and set aside for 10 minutes. Run a knife around the edge of the soufflés and turn them out onto a wire rack.

To make the Parmesan glaze, whisk the cream, Parmesan and egg yolks until combined. To make the apple and walnut salad, toss together the frisée, watercress, apple and chives. Add the walnuts, a splash of red wine vinegar, a good drizzle of olive oil, salt and freshly ground black pepper.

Place the soufflés upside down on a baking tray lined with baking paper and bake for 10 minutes. Coat the tops of the soufflés with the Parmesan glaze. Grill (broil) under a medium grill (broiler) until the tops are golden. To serve, use a spatula to gently lift the soufflés onto serving plates and serve immediately with the salad.

to drink
Allan Scott Riesling, Marlborough, New Zealand
Natural fruit sweetness and acidity create a wonderful platform for this delicately rich soufflé.

grilled prawns and panzanella salad

36 large raw prawns (shrimp), peeled and deveined,
  tails intact
125 ml (4 fl oz/^{1}/$_2$ cup) olive oil
1 red chilli, roughly chopped
2 garlic cloves, crushed
1 teaspoon coriander seeds, roasted and crushed
olive oil
6 lemon or lime wedges

Red wine vinaigrette
1 garlic clove, crushed
juice of ^{1}/$_4$ lemon
50 ml (1^3/$_4$ fl oz) red wine vinegar
150 ml (5 fl oz) extra virgin olive oil

Panzanella salad
2 red capsicums (peppers)
2 yellow capsicums (peppers)
olive oil
6 vine-ripened tomatoes, blanched and peeled
1 red onion, thinly sliced
1 red chilli, finely chopped
a handful of basil, leaves picked and washed
90 g (3^1/$_4$ oz/^{1}/$_2$ cup) Ligurian or Kalamata olives
8 anchovy fillets, drained and halved lengthwise
1 teaspoon salted capers, rinsed
^{1}/$_2$ loaf ciabatta, cut into large dice, toasted

Serves 6

Soak twelve bamboo skewers in water for 30 minutes. Thread three prawns on each skewer. Combine the oil, chilli, garlic and coriander seeds and season with salt and freshly ground black pepper. Pour the marinade over the prawns, cover and refrigerate for at least 2 hours, preferably overnight.

To make the red wine vinaigrette, whisk the garlic, lemon juice, vinegar and olive oil until combined.

To make the panzanella salad, preheat the oven to 250°C (500°F/Gas 9). Wash and dry the capsicums and rub well with olive oil. Put on a baking tray and roast until the skin is well blistered, turning once or twice. Transfer the capsicums to a bowl, cover with plastic wrap and set aside to cool. Peel off the skin and discard it along with the seeds and membrane. Slice the capsicums into medium-sized strips.

Halve the tomatoes horizontally, then quarter each half. Combine the tomato with the capsicum, onion, chilli, basil, olives, anchovies and capers in a large bowl. Toss lightly, then add the bread and enough of the red wine vinaigrette to moisten the salad.

Heat a barbecue or ridged grill pan to high heat and brush with olive oil. Cook the prawns on both sides until pink and opaque.

To serve, arrange the salad on serving plates, top with the prawn skewers and serve with a wedge of lemon or lime.

to drink
Bannockburn Saignee, Geelong, Victoria
A light Tuscan bread salad nicely matched with a chilled rosé style wine.

barbecued whiting fillets with shaved fennel and watercress

18–24 whiting fillets
2 small fennel bulbs, outer leaves removed
100 g (3$^{1}/_{2}$ oz) watercress, stems removed, washed
50 g (1$^{3}/_{4}$ oz/1 cup) celery leaves (inner pale leaves)
1 tablespoon picked and washed chive leaves
1 teaspoon wholegrain mustard
grated zest and juice of 1 lemon
1 tablespoon extra virgin olive oil
plain (all-purpose) flour, for dusting
125 g (4$^{1}/_{2}$ oz) clarified butter
6 lemon wedges

Roasted garlic mayonnaise
1 bulb of garlic, cloves separated, unpeeled
olive oil
2 egg yolks
2 teaspoons Dijon mustard
2 tablespoons white wine vinegar
juice of $^{1}/_{2}$ lemon, or to taste
250 ml (9 fl oz/1 cup) extra virgin olive oil
250 ml (9 fl oz/1 cup) olive oil
a pinch of cayenne pepper

Serves 6

To make the roasted garlic mayonnaise, preheat the oven to 160°C (315°F/Gas 2–3). Put the garlic on a sheet of aluminium foil, drizzle liberally with olive oil and fold up loosely. Bake on a baking tray for 30–40 minutes, or until the garlic is tender.

Put the egg yolks, mustard, vinegar and lemon juice in a food processor and process until smooth. With the motor running, slowly add the combined oils until the mayonnaise is thick and well blended. If it is too thick, add a little hot water. Transfer the mayonnaise to a bowl and whisk in the cayenne pepper and a little salt. Squeeze the cooked garlic from the cloves and roughly chop the flesh. Fold the garlic through the mayonnaise. If necessary, add a little extra lemon juice, to taste. (This makes approximately 500 g (1lb 2 oz/2 cups). Store in the refrigerator in an airtight container.)

Prepare the whiting fillets by running your finger on the underside of the fillet to locate the bones and cutting a neat 'V' shaped incision to loosen them. Lift the bones out carefully.

Use a mandolin or sharp knife to finely shave the fennel. Combine the fennel with the watercress, celery leaves and chives. Combine the mustard, lemon juice, lemon zest and olive oil and season with salt and freshly ground black pepper. Drizzle over the fennel mixture and lightly toss.

Heat a barbecue flat plate to high heat. Season the flour with salt and freshly ground black pepper. Dust the whiting fillets with flour, then brush with clarified butter. Sear the fish, skin side down, until golden brown. Turn and briefly cook the other side. To serve, arrange the fish on serving plates and top with the fennel mixture. Accompany with the roasted garlic mayonnaise and lemon wedges.

to drink
Mitchelton Airstrip Marsanne Roussanne Viognier, Victoria
This traditional Rhône-style white blend has stone fruit characters that make it a perfect wine for food.

chicken with goat's cheese, semi-dried tomatoes and coriander

I can remember serving this dish in my first restaurant in the late 1980s (showing my age a bit), and I'm still not over it, so I guess you could say it's stood the test of time.

6 medium chicken supremes, skin on
100 g (3^1/$_2$ oz) goat's cheese
12 semi-dried (sun-blushed) tomatoes
a small handful of coriander (cilantro), picked into
   sprigs and washed
dressed mixed leaves, to serve

Serves 6

Carefully lift the skin from the bone end of each chicken supreme and make a pocket. Put 1 tablespoon of goat's cheese in the pocket and then put 2 semi-dried tomatoes on the goat's cheese. Add a few sprigs of coriander. Pull the skin down over the filling. Cover and refrigerate until required.

Preheat the oven to 180°C (350°F/Gas 4). Heat a barbecue chargrill or flat plate to medium-high heat. Season the chicken with salt and freshly ground black pepper. Seal the chicken on both sides, then transfer to the oven and cook for 10–12 minutes, or until the chicken is cooked through. Serve with the dressed mixed leaves.

to drink
Wirra Wirra Chardonnay, Adelaide Hills, South Australia
Cool climate chardonnay is a great partner for white meats such as chicken and pork.

moroccan-spiced barbecue quail

North African flavours have become very popular over the last few years, and after you've tried this quail you will certainly know why — they're delicious!

6 boned and butterflied quails (see glossary)
sea salt

Moroccan marinade
125 ml (4 fl oz/1/2 cup) olive oil
1 tablespoon honey
2 star anise
a few thyme sprigs, leaves picked and washed
2 garlic cloves, sliced

1 teaspoon paprika
a good grind of black pepper
a large pinch of ground cumin
a large pinch of ground coriander
2 cinnamon sticks, broken
a large pinch of chilli flakes
a pinch of saffron threads (optional)

Serves 6

To make the Moroccan marinade, combine all the ingredients. Pour the marinade over the quails, cover and refrigerate overnight.

Soak twelve bamboo skewers in water for 30 minutes. Drain the marinade from the quails. Push two skewers through each quail diagonally across each other so that the quail sits flat — this will make it easier for cooking and turning on the barbecue.

Heat a barbecue chargrill to high heat. Put the quails on the barbecue and season with sea salt. Using the skewers, turn the quails several times until they are cooked through and evenly coloured on both sides. Press the quails down with tongs so the skin will brown. This dish is nice served with couscous and harissa.

to drink
Coriole Sangiovese, McLaren Vale, South Australia
This Tuscan chianti grape shows chocolate and liquorice characters, adding an extra dimension to the North African spices.

Attention to detail is my obsession — but after that,

I try to do the very least with the very best of produce.

smoked trout, baby beets, horseradish and beetroot grissini

This is a variation of a dish by a good friend of mine, Darren Simpson. It is the epitome of simplicity, letting the flavours and colours speak for themselves.

12 baby beets, trimmed
1/2 bulb of garlic, roughly chopped
a few thyme sprigs, leaves picked and washed
100 g (3 1/2 oz) rocket (arugula), stems
   removed, washed
450 g (1 lb) smoked trout, skin and bones removed
1 small fresh horseradish, peeled (optional)

Horseradish crème fraîche
1 teaspoon Dijon mustard
1 tablespoon horseradish cream
185 ml (6 fl oz/3/4 cup) crème fraîche
grated zest of 1 lemon

Beetroot grissini
250 g (9 oz/2 cups) plain (all-purpose) flour, sifted
1 teaspoon salt
2 teaspoons dried yeast
1 tablespoon honey
1 tablespoon olive oil
125 ml (4 fl oz/1/2 cup) fresh or canned beetroot juice
olive oil, extra
sea salt

Serves 6

Preheat the oven to 170°C (325°F/Gas 3). To prepare the baby beets, wash the beets and put in a large bowl with the garlic and thyme. Toss together with a good drizzle of olive oil, salt and freshly ground black pepper. Spread the mixture on a non-stick baking tray, splash with a little water and cover with aluminium foil. Bake for 45–50 minutes, or until the beets are tender when pierced with a knife. Let cool, then cut the beets in half.

Meanwhile, to make the beetroot grissini, combine the flour, salt and yeast in a food processor. Combine the honey, oil and beetroot juice, then add to the dry ingredients in the processor. Pulse until combined, then transfer to a floured surface. Knead four or five times, just long enough to bring together. Cut the dough into walnut-sized pieces and roll into pencil-thin strips, 15–20 cm (6–8 inches) long. Rest for 10 minutes.

Place the grissini on a non-stick baking tray or a baking tray lined with baking paper, brush with olive oil and season with sea salt and freshly ground black pepper. Bake for 15 minutes, or until crisp and golden.

To make the horseradish crème fraîche, whisk the mustard and horseradish cream into the crème fraîche. Add the grated lemon zest, salt and freshly ground black pepper. Thin with a little hot water, if necessary, to achieve a drizzling consistency. To serve, scatter rocket leaves over the serving plates and place four beet halves on top. Arrange the smoked trout around the salad, then grate the fresh horseradish over the top, if using. Drizzle over the horseradish crème fraîche. Finish with a good grind of black pepper. Serve with the beetroot grissini.

to drink
Turkey Flat Rosé, Barossa Valley, South Australia
For Sunday afternoons grazing on the back deck with friends, you can't beat a delicate, slightly sweet rosé.

seared salmon, bok choy, chilli and lime

If you make the dressing in advance, this is a 10–15 minute dish, but the end result is so clean, fresh and vibrant nobody will know how easy it is to prepare.

6 x 175 g (6 oz) salmon fillets, skin on, pin-boned
  (see glossary)
olive oil
9 baby bok choy (pak choi), halved and outer
  leaves removed
6 lime halves, to serve

Chilli, lime and palm sugar dressing
2 tablespoons peanut or vegetable oil
2 tablespoons black or brown mustard seeds
2 garlic cloves, thinly sliced
3 large red chillies, sliced on the diagonal
25 g (1 oz/$1/3$ cup) julienned fresh ginger
125 g ($4^1/2$ oz) palm sugar, grated
2 teaspoons fish sauce
juice of 6 limes

Serves 6

To make the chilli, lime and palm sugar dressing, heat the oil in a small saucepan until very hot. Add the mustard seeds and cook for 2–3 seconds, or until they begin to pop. Add the garlic and cook until golden and beginning to crisp. Add the chilli and ginger and cook for a further 1–2 minutes. Remove from the heat and add the palm sugar, fish sauce and lime juice, to taste.

Season the salmon skin with salt and freshly ground black pepper. Heat a non-stick frying pan over high heat and add a little olive oil. Sear the salmon, skin side down, until golden brown. Reduce the heat to medium, turn the salmon over and cook for 3–5 minutes for medium rare.

Blanch the bok choy in a large saucepan of boiling water until tender, then drain.

To serve, divide the bok choy among serving plates, top with the salmon and drizzle with the dressing. Serve with the lime halves.

to drink
Lime and mint granita
The refreshing flavours of crushed ice, lime and mint both clean and cool the palate. To make, put 6–8 ice cubes (about 1 cup), the segments of $1/2$ lime, a small handful of mint leaves and a dash of sugar syrup (see essentials) in a blender. Blend briefly to crush the ice, then serve in a tall glass.

lamb loin with eggplant, watercress, salted lemon and chilli

2 small eggplants (aubergines), cut into 1.5 cm
  (5/8 inch) slices
olive oil
3 x 200 g (7 oz) lamb loins, trimmed of fat and
  silver skin

Balsamic vinaigrette
60 ml (2 fl oz/1/4 cup) balsamic vinegar
1 garlic clove, finely chopped
a pinch of caster (superfine) sugar
185 ml (6 fl oz/3/4 cup) olive oil
2 thyme sprigs, leaves picked and washed

Watercress salad
300 g (10 1/2 oz/1 bunch) watercress, stems
  removed, washed
85 g (3 oz/1 bunch) coriander (cilantro), leaves picked
  and washed
1 red chilli, seeded and cut into strips
1 red onion, sliced
rind of 1/2 salted lemon or preserved lemon, cut into
  strips (see essentials)

Serves 6

Preheat a grill (broiler) or barbecue chargrill to high heat. Lightly brush the eggplant with olive oil and cook for 5–8 minutes, or until tender and browned. Keep warm.

Preheat the oven to 220°C (425°F/Gas 7). Brush the lamb with olive oil and season with salt and freshly ground black pepper. Heat a frying pan over high heat and seal the lamb on both sides until browned. Transfer the lamb to a baking tray and bake for 10–12 minutes for medium. Set aside to rest for 5 minutes before slicing.

Meanwhile, to make the balsamic vinaigrette, whisk the vinegar, garlic, sugar, oil and thyme leaves until combined. Season to taste with salt and freshly ground black pepper.

To make the salad, combine the watercress, coriander, chilli, onion and salted lemon or preserved lemon rind. Add enough of the balsamic vinaigrette to moisten the salad.

To serve, place two to three slices of eggplant on each serving plate. Slice each lamb loin into discs, about 5 mm (1/4 inch) thick, and toss through the salad. Arrange the salad over the eggplant. Finish with a light drizzle of extra balsamic vinaigrette.

to drink
Wyndam Estate Bin 5555 Shiraz, Hunter Valley, New South Wales
Hunter Valley shiraz is earthy and savoury; exactly what is needed for barbecued lamb and smoky eggplant.

sumac-spiced lamb with pumpkin, fennel and hummus

6 x 3-cutlet lamb racks, trimmed (leaving a little fat)
3 garlic cloves, crushed
2 rosemary sprigs, leaves picked and washed
grated zest of $1/2$ lemon
olive oil
1.5 kg (3 lb 5 oz) pumpkin, cut into 6 wedges
extra virgin olive oil
2 teaspoons cumin seeds, roasted and ground
2 pinches of sumac
jus, demi-glace or veal glaze, to serve (see essentials)

Hummus
225 g (8 oz/1 cup) chickpeas, soaked in water overnight
6–8 garlic cloves, unpeeled
olive oil

juice of $1/2$ lemon
2 teaspoons white wine vinegar
2 teaspoons tahini
60 ml (2 fl oz/$1/4$ cup) extra virgin olive oil

Fennel and parsley salad
4 baby fennel bulbs, thinly sliced lengthwise
$1/2$ red onion, thinly sliced
a small handful of flat-leaf (Italian) parsley, leaves
   picked, washed and coarsely chopped
1 tablespoon lemon juice
1 tablespoon wholegrain mustard
extra virgin olive oil

Serves 6

Marinate the lamb overnight in a non-metallic dish with the garlic, rosemary, lemon zest and a splash of olive oil. To make the hummus, drain the chickpeas and transfer to a saucepan. Cover with water and bring to the boil. Simmer for 1 hour, or until tender. Remove from the heat, allow to cool, then drain, reserving the cooking liquid.

Preheat the oven to 160°C (315°F/Gas 2–3). Put the garlic on a sheet of aluminium foil, drizzle liberally with olive oil and fold up loosely. Bake on a baking tray for 30–40 minutes, or until tender. When cool, squeeze the garlic flesh from the skins. Put the chickpeas, lemon juice, vinegar, tahini, garlic flesh, salt and freshly ground black pepper in a food processor and process briefly to combine. With the motor running, slowly add the extra virgin olive oil. Adjust the consistency with a little of the reserved cooking liquid. Season to taste.

To make the fennel and parsley salad, combine the shaved fennel, onion and parsley in a bowl. Add the lemon juice and mustard and mix lightly, adding enough extra virgin olive oil to moisten the salad. Season.

Increase the heat to 200°C (400°F/Gas 6). Put the pumpkin wedges on a baking tray lined with baking paper. Drizzle with a little extra virgin olive oil and season with the cumin, salt and freshly ground black pepper. Bake for 40 minutes, or until tender. Set aside and keep warm. Increase the oven to 220°C (425°F/Gas 7). Heat a wide ovenproof frying pan over high heat. Wipe the marinade from the lamb racks with paper towels. Season the lamb and seal on both sides. Transfer the pan to the oven and cook the lamb for 15–20 minutes for medium. Rest in a warm place for 5 minutes. To serve, slice the lamb racks into cutlets. Place a wedge of pumpkin on one side of each serving plate with a handful of the salad and a spoonful of hummus alongside. Place the cutlets next to the salad, sprinkle with sumac and drizzle the lamb with the warm jus.

to drink
Zema Estate Cabernet Sauvignon, Merlot, Cabernet Franc, Malbec, Coonawarra, South Australia
A top-flight Coonawarra cabernet is an ideal companion to sweetly spiced lamb and pumpkin.

tempura barramundi, thai herb salad and naam jim

oil, for deep-frying
600 g (1 lb 5 oz) barramundi fillets, or other skinless
    white-fleshed fish, cut into 1 cm (1/2 inch) thick
    fingers
plain (all-purpose) flour, for dusting
sea salt

Thai herb salad
2 French shallots, thinly sliced
2 spring onions (scallions), thinly sliced
2 red chillies, seeded and thinly sliced
a small handful of Vietnamese mint, leaves picked
    and washed
a small handful of coriander (cilantro), leaves picked
    and washed

Tempura batter
1 egg
a pinch of bicarbonate of soda
90 g (3 1/4 oz/3/4 cup) plain (all-purpose) flour

Naam jim
2 red chillies, seeded
1 garlic clove
2 coriander roots
1 small knob galangal, peeled and chopped
15 g (1/2 oz) light palm sugar, grated
125 ml (4 fl oz/1/2 cup) lime juice
1 tablespoon fish sauce

Serves 6

To make the naam jim, use a mortar and pestle to pound the chilli, garlic, coriander and galangal until smooth and well combined. Add the palm sugar, lime juice and fish sauce, to taste — the sauce should taste hot, sour and sweet, in that order.

To make the tempura batter, whisk the egg, 250 ml (9 fl oz/1 cup) water, bicarbonate of soda and flour to make a smooth batter.

Heat the oil in a deep-fat fryer or large saucepan to 190°C (375°F), or until a piece of bread fries golden brown in 10 seconds when dropped into the oil. Dust the barramundi fingers with flour, shake off the excess, then dip into the tempura batter. Fry the barramundi in batches until crisp and golden. Drain on paper towels and season with sea salt.

To make the Thai herb salad, toss the shallots, spring onion, chilli and herbs to combine. To serve, divide the salad among plates with the tempura barramundi fingers alongside and the naam jim for dipping.

to drink
Houghton's Chenin Blanc, Western Australia
Passionfruit, pineapple and citrus, with just a hint of sweetness to finish. Sounds just like Thai cooking.

coral trout, asian greens, shiitake and tamarind and chilli sauce

6 x 175 g (6 oz) coral trout fillets, or other firm, white-fleshed fish, skin on, pin-boned (see glossary)

1 tablespoon unsalted butter

50 g (1$^3/_4$ oz/1 cup) dried shiitake mushrooms

2 teaspoons caster (superfine) sugar

1$^1/_2$ tablespoons soy sauce

450 g (1 lb/2 bunches) broccolini

600 g (1 lb 5 oz/2 bunches) choy sum

4 baby bok choy (pak choi)

3 cm (1$^1/_4$ in) piece ginger, julienned

3 garlic cloves, sliced

2 tablespoons Chinese black olive and mustard (available from Chinatown food stores)

Tamarind and chilli sauce

70 g (2$^1/_2$ oz) tamarind

olive oil

3 red onions, diced

4 medium red chillies, finely diced

4 garlic cloves, finely chopped

150 g (5$^1/_2$ oz) palm sugar, grated

1 heaped tablespoon dried shrimp

fish sauce

lime juice

Serves 6

To make the tamarind and chilli sauce, soak the tamarind in warm water to form a smooth paste. Pass the tamarind through a coarse sieve, reserving the liquid. Heat a little olive oil in a frying pan over medium heat and sauté the onion, chilli and garlic, without colouring, until tender. Add the palm sugar and cook until the mixture is sticky. Using a mortar and pestle, crush the dried shrimp. Add the shrimp and tamarind pulp to the onion mixture. Adjust the consistency with the reserved tamarind water. Add the fish sauce and lime juice, to taste.

Score the skin of the coral trout with a sharp knife and season with salt and pepper. Heat a little olive oil in a frying pan over high heat. Cook the trout, skin side down, until golden brown. Reduce the heat, turn the trout over and cook the other side. When the fish is nearly cooked, remove from the heat. Add the butter to the pan.

Meanwhile, put the shiitake mushrooms in a bowl. Dissolve the sugar in a little warm water, add the soy sauce and pour over the mushrooms, adding more water if necessary to cover the mushrooms. Set aside to soak for 5 minutes, then drain the mushrooms, reserving the soaking liquid. Chop the mushrooms.

Blanch the broccolini, choy sum and bok choy in boiling salted water. Heat a frying pan over high heat, add the ginger, garlic, Chinese black olive and mustard, shiitake mushrooms and a little of the soaking liquid and cook briefly. Add the blanched Asian greens and season to taste with salt and freshly ground black pepper.

To serve, place the Asian greens and mushrooms with some of the sauce in the centre of each serving plate and rest the fish on top. Deglaze the pan the vegetables were cooked in with the tamarind and chilli sauce and heat through. Spoon the warm sauce over and around the fish.

to drink
Spring Vale Gewürztraminer, Tasmania
Musk and rosewater, with a little residual sweetness, make gewürztraminer a great match for Asian ingredients.

grilled white fish with green olive salsa and chunky fries

6 large potatoes, unpeeled
oil, for deep-frying
plain (all-purpose) flour, for dusting
6 x 175 g (6 oz) white fish fillets, such as barramundi,
   snapper or blue-eye cod
clarified butter, melted (see essentials)

Green olive salsa
1 small red onion, diced
rind of 1 salted lemon or preserved lemon, diced
   (see essentials)
2 tablespoons salted capers, rinsed
90 g (3¼ oz/½ cup) green olives, sliced
juice and grated zest of 1 lemon
1 teaspoon extra virgin olive oil

Serves 6

Steam the potatoes until tender. Allow to cool, then refrigerate overnight.

To make the green olive salsa, combine the onion, salted lemon or preserved lemon rind, capers, olives, lemon juice, lemon zest and olive oil. Season to taste with salt and freshly ground black pepper.

Peel the potatoes and cut them into thick fries. Heat the oil in a deep-fat fryer or large saucepan to 180°C (350°F), or until a piece of bread fries golden brown in 15 seconds when dropped into the oil. Cook the fries in batches until crisp and golden. Drain on paper towels.

Preheat a grill (broiler) to hot. Season the flour with salt and freshly ground black pepper. Either halve the fish fillets or leave them whole, then dust with the flour and shake off the excess. Put the fish on a greased baking tray, brush with clarified butter and season with salt and freshly ground black pepper. Grill (broil) the fish for 8–10 minutes, or until just cooked and golden.

To serve, place the fish on serving plates with the fries alongside. Add a spoonful of green olive salsa.

to drink
Saltram Semillon, Barossa Valley, South Australia
The fresh characters of lime and cut grass accentuate the intensity of the olive salsa without overpowering the delicacy of the fish.

chicken wrapped in prosciutto with sage and garlic

3 small bulbs of garlic, cloves separated, unpeeled
olive oil
6 skinless chicken breast fillets
a handful of sage, leaves picked and washed
12 slices prosciutto
500 g (1 lb 2 oz) butterbeans (lima beans), stalks
   removed, left whole
1 tablespoon unsalted butter
1–2 tablespoons wholegrain mustard, to serve
jus, demi-glace or veal glaze, to serve (see essentials)

Parmesan potatoes
6 medium potatoes, such as sebago
2 tablespoons extra virgin olive oil
2 tablespoons picked, washed and chopped
   thyme leaves
3 garlic cloves, finely chopped
100 g (3^1/$_2$ oz/1 cup) grated Parmesan cheese

Mustard cream
125 ml (4 fl oz/^{1}/$_2$ cup) crème fraîche
1 tablespoon Dijon mustard
1 tablespoon wholegrain mustard
juice of ^{1}/$_2$ lemon

Serves 6

Preheat the oven to 160°C (315°F/Gas 2–3). Put the garlic on a sheet of aluminium foil, drizzle with olive oil and fold up loosely. Bake on a baking tray for 30–40 minutes, or until the garlic is tender. Set aside to cool.

To make the Parmesan potatoes, increase the oven to 200°C (400°F/Gas 6). Wash the potatoes and slice them into 1 cm (^{1}/$_2$ inch) rounds. Put the potato in a bowl and toss with the olive oil, thyme and garlic. Spread the potato on a baking tray lined with baking paper and season with salt and freshly ground black pepper. Bake for 20 minutes, or until tender. Preheat a grill (broiler) to medium. Sprinkle the potato with the Parmesan and grill (broil) until golden. Set aside until needed.

Squeeze the flesh from the garlic cloves and put several cloves on each chicken breast. Top with three to four sage leaves and a grind of black pepper, then wrap the chicken with the prosciutto, covering the whole breast.

Heat a little olive oil in a heavy-based frying pan over medium heat. Seal the chicken on both sides and transfer to a baking tray. With the oven still at 200°C (400°F/Gas 6), bake for 12–15 minutes, or until the chicken is cooked but still moist. Allow it to rest for 5 minutes. Meanwhile, blanch the butterbeans in a saucepan of boiling salted water until tender. Drain well, season and toss with the butter. Next, make the mustard cream. Combine the crème fraîche, mustards and lemon juice.

To serve, reheat the potato and divide among serving plates. Slice the chicken breasts and arrange beside the potato. Arrange the beans next to the chicken and potato. Top the beans with a tablespoon of mustard cream, then a teaspoon of wholegrain mustard. Drizzle the warm jus over and around.

to drink
Yalumba Viognier, Eden Valley, New South Wales
This dish demands a wine with enough texture to stand up to its powerful flavours. Viognier is more than capable.

osso bucco, buttered beans and mash

plain (all-purpose) flour, for dusting

12 osso bucco, 7–8 cm (2³/4–3¹/4 inches) across, 2 cm (³/4 inch) thick

olive oil

2 onions, finely diced

3 garlic cloves, thinly sliced

2 carrots, peeled and diced

2 celery stalks, diced

1 leek, white part only, finely diced

250 ml (9 fl oz/1 cup) white wine

400 g (14 oz) tin tomatoes, diced and juice reserved

2 tablespoons tomato paste (purée)

1–1.5 litres (35–52 fl oz/4–6 cups) beef stock

300 g (10¹/2 oz) French beans, trimmed

1 tablespoon unsalted butter

Mash

1.25 kg (2 lb 12 oz) pink-skinned waxy potatoes, such as desiree, peeled and diced

250 ml (9 fl oz/1 cup) milk

125 ml (4 fl oz/¹/2 cup) cream

125 g (4¹/2 oz) unsalted butter, cubed

Gremolata

a large handful of flat-leaf (Italian) parsley, leaves picked, washed and finely chopped

zest of 2 lemons

2 garlic cloves, chopped

Serves 6

Preheat the oven to 180°C (350°F/Gas 4). Season the flour with salt and freshly ground black pepper. Lightly coat the osso bucco in the flour, then shake off the excess. Heat some olive oil in a frying pan over high heat. Seal the osso bucco well in batches, transferring to a large flameproof casserole as they brown.

Add the onion, garlic, carrot, celery and leek to the frying pan and cook until golden. Transfer the vegetables to the casserole with the osso bucco. Deglaze the pan with the wine, stirring to loosen the sediment. Add the chopped tomato, reserved tomato juice and tomato paste. Cook for several minutes, then pour the tomato mixture into the casserole with enough of the beef stock to cover the osso bucco and vegetables. Bake, covered, for 1–1¹/2 hours, or until the meat is tender and pulls away from the bone.

To make the mash, cook the potato in a large saucepan of boiling salted water until just tender. Drain well. Pass the potato through a mouli, or mash. Put the milk, cream and butter in a saucepan, bring to the boil, then gradually stir into the potato, adding enough of the mixture to achieve a light, smooth consistency. Season with salt and freshly ground black pepper. To make the gremolata, combine the parsley, lemon zest and garlic.

Blanch the beans in a saucepan of boiling salted water, drain well, then toss with the butter, salt and freshly ground black pepper. To serve, put a large spoonful of hot mash in the centre of each serving plate. Rest the beans alongside, top with two osso bucco, then spoon the sauce over. Scatter the gremolata over and serve.

to drink
Rosemount GSM (Grenache, Shiraz, Mourvedre), McLaren Vale, South Australia
A classic Australian for a classic dish.

What makes a dish special to me is whether it looks as

appealing today as it ever did.

roast pork with apple and sichuan pepper relish

2–2.25 kg (4 lb 8 oz–5 lb) pork loin, boned, skin on,
   rolled and scored
olive oil
12 stems broccolini

Apple and Sichuan pepper relish
olive oil
1/2 brown onion, finely diced
2 garlic cloves, finely chopped
4 Granny Smith apples, peeled and chopped

1/4–1/2 teaspoon Sichuan pepper, roasted and
   crushed, or to taste (see note)
90 g (3 1/4 oz/1/2 cup) soft brown sugar
grated zest of 1 orange
80 ml (2 1/2 fl oz/1/3 cup) cider or sherry vinegar
sea salt
1 tablespoon mustard seeds
1 tablespoon picked, washed and chopped
   marjoram leaves

Serves 6

To make the apple and Sichuan pepper relish, heat some olive oil in a saucepan over medium heat. Sauté the onion and garlic, without browning, until the onion is translucent. Add the apple, Sichuan pepper, brown sugar, orange zest, vinegar and 250 ml (9 fl oz/1 cup) water. Season with sea salt and bring to the boil. Reduce the heat and simmer for 20–25 minutes, or until the apple begins to soften. Cool slightly, then stir through the mustard seeds and chopped marjoram.

Preheat the oven to 220°C (425°F/Gas 7). Put the pork on a roasting rack in a baking tray. Rub the pork rind with some olive oil and then liberally rub with salt. Bake for 30 minutes, then reduce the oven temperature to 180°C (350°F/Gas 4) and bake for a further 1 1/4 hours. Rest the pork for 10–15 minutes before serving.

Steam or blanch the broccolini in boiling salted water. To serve, slice the pork and arrange on plates with the broccolini and a spoonful of apple and Sichuan relish alongside. Store any leftover relish in an airtight container in the refrigerator.

note
Sichuan pepper is native to the Sichuan province of China. Although it bears some resemblance to black peppercorns, it isn't actually from the pepper family but is a dried berry from a tree of the prickly ash family. It is sometimes referred to as anise pepper, and has a mild, peppery, citrus bouquet and flavour.

to drink
Edward & Chaffey Cabernet Sauvignon, McLaren Vale, South Australia
Spice, violets and a hint of green leaf dominate this cabernet, making it a perfect foil for the sweet and peppery flavours of the dish.

roast duck, pommes écrasées and balsamic radicchio

2 x 1.8 kg (4 lb) ducks
2 oranges, roughly chopped
1 bulb of garlic, cut in half
10 g (1/4 oz/1/2 bunch) thyme, leaves picked
    and washed
jus, demi-glace or veal glaze, to serve (see essentials)

Pommes écrasées
6 medium desiree potatoes
rock salt (optional)
1 tablespoon unsalted butter
a small handful of flat-leaf (Italian) parsley, leaves
    picked, washed and roughly chopped
4 rashers of bacon, grilled (broiled) and chopped

Balsamic radicchio
3 small tight heads of radicchio
olive oil
1 tablespoon unsalted butter
balsamic vinegar
1–2 tablespoons soft brown sugar

Serves 6

Preheat the oven to 220°C (425°F/Gas 7). Season the cavity of each duck with salt and black pepper. Fill each duck with orange pieces, 1/2 bulb of garlic and thyme leaves. Put the ducks on a wire rack over a tray to allow any fat to drain off during cooking. Roast the ducks for 11/4–11/2 hours, or until cooked through. When the ducks are cool enough to handle, cut them into large pieces. Cut the breasts and legs in half.

To make the pommes écrasées, reduce the oven to 180°C (350°F/Gas 4). Bake the potatoes on a wire rack or a baking tray lined with rock salt for 45–50 minutes, or until tender when pierced with a knife. Set aside until cool enough to handle.

Meanwhile, to make the balsamic radicchio, cut each head of radicchio into six wedges. Heat a little olive oil in a frying pan over high heat. Add the radicchio, salt and freshly ground black pepper and sauté for 2 minutes. Add the butter, a splash of balsamic vinegar and brown sugar, to taste. Reduce the heat and cook, covered, until the radicchio has softened. Remove the pan from the heat and fold through the bacon.

Scoop out the potato flesh and discard the skins. Season the potato with salt and freshly ground black pepper, then add the butter, parsley and bacon. Fold through, retaining some texture.

To serve, briefly reheat the duck pieces under a hot grill (broiler). Divide the pommes écrasées and radicchio among serving plates, rest a duck breast and leg on the leaves and drizzle over and around with warm jus.

to drink
Yalumba Cabernet Sauvignon Shiraz, Barossa Valley, South Australia
Yalumba has been producing quality wine in the Barossa Valley for 150 years and, with dollops of red berries and currants, this one is no exception.

thai-spiced snapper with warm potato salad

Cooking fish by this method has two advantages. Firstly, it can be prepared in advance. Secondly, it's so effective at sealing in all the flavours that it's one of those dishes I love — maximum flavour with minimum effort.

6 plate-sized fish, cleaned, such as snapper, parrot
   fish, baby barramundi, coral trout or sweetlip
olive oil

Thai spices
20 g (3/4 oz/1/4 cup) julienned fresh ginger
30 g (1 oz/1/3 cup) red chillies, seeded and julienned
1 lemongrass stalk, white part only, thinly sliced
   or crushed
juice and grated zest of 2 limes
juice and grated zest of 2 lemons
6 garlic cloves, thinly sliced
1 tablespoon peanut or vegetable oil

Potato salad
12 small potatoes
extra virgin olive oil
juice of 1–2 lemons
1 heaped tablespoon wholegrain mustard
a small handful of chives, leaves picked, washed
   and chopped
a handful of flat-leaf (Italian) parsley, leaves picked
   and washed
6 rashers of bacon, grilled (broiled), roughly chopped

Serves 6

To make the potato salad, steam or boil the potatoes until tender. Cut in half while still warm and put in a large serving bowl. Drizzle with extra virgin olive oil and lemon juice. Season with salt and freshly ground black pepper. Set aside for the potato to absorb the flavours.

To make the Thai spices, combine all the ingredients in a bowl.

Using a sharp knife, make several incisions diagonally across both sides of each fish. Rub the fish with olive oil and season with salt and freshly ground black pepper. Put each fish on a large sheet of aluminium foil, folded over for double thickness.

Spoon the Thai spices evenly over the fish. Wrap the fish in the foil and bake on a hot barbecue flat plate for 5 minutes on each side. Rest for 5 minutes before serving.

To serve, add the mustard, chives, parsley and bacon to the potato. Place the fish on serving plates and serve the potato salad separately.

to drink
Mills Reef Reserve Gewürztraminer, Gisborne, New Zealand
Intense, spicy lychee and citrus add an amazing extra dimension to this dining experience.

pommes anna

Peel 1.5 kg (3 lb 5 oz) potatoes and thinly slice using a mandolin or a sharp knife. Heat a 28 cm (11 inch) non-stick ovenproof frying pan over medium heat. Brush the base of the pan with a generous amount of melted clarified butter, approximately 50 g (1^3/4 oz/^{1}/4 cup), then arrange a layer of overlapping slices of potato to cover the base. Using a pastry brush, brush with a little more clarified butter and lightly season with salt and freshly ground black pepper. Arrange another layer of overlapping slices of potato on top, brush with clarified butter and season. Repeat this process until the pan is full. By this time, the base should be evenly coloured.

Transfer to preheated 180°C (350°F/Gas 4) oven and cook for 40–50 minutes, or until the potato is tender when pierced with a knife.

Press the potato down with a flat plate or tray and top with a weight, if necessary, to gently compress the potato so that the pommes anna will hold together once cut. Cool in the pan, still covered, for 15–20 minutes before turning out onto a wire rack. To serve, cut wedges of pommes anna and reheat if necessary. Serves 8

note
Pommes anna go nicely with most grilled (broiled) meats and poultry.

fennel à la grecque

Trim the outside leaves from 3 large or 6 baby fennel bulbs. Cut each bulb into 6–8 wedges, depending on the size of the fennel (if using baby fennel bulbs, cut them in half).

Pour 1 litre (35 fl oz/4 cups) water into a saucepan and add 125 ml (4 fl oz/^{1}/2 cup) olive oil, the juice of 2 lemons, 3 bay leaves, a few washed thyme sprigs, 1 teaspoon coriander seeds, a few black peppercorns and a good pinch of salt. Bring to the boil, then add the fennel. Cover with baking paper and a small plate to keep the fennel submerged during cooking. Simmer gently for 10–15 minutes, or until the fennel is tender. Allow the fennel to cool in the cooking liquid. Serve the fennel with some of the cooking liquid spooned over. Serves 8

note
Serve at room temperature with grilled (broiled) seafood such as salmon or prawns (shrimp), or as a side dish.

steamed broccoli and feta

Cut 2 large heads of broccoli into florets. Blanch them in a saucepan of boiling salted water. Drain the broccoli and toss with a little extra virgin olive oil, salt and freshly ground black pepper. To serve, put the broccoli in a serving bowl and crumble 150 g (5^1/2 oz) feta over the top. Serves 6 as an accompaniment

corn bread

Baking bread demands confidence, but it can be very rewarding and not as difficult as you think. And, there's nothing nicer than a house that smells of freshly baked bread.

$2^1/2$ teaspoons dried yeast
a pinch of sugar
450 g (1 lb/3 cups) strong bread flour, sifted
115 g (4 oz/$^3/4$ cup) polenta
1 tablespoon unsalted butter

375 ml (11 fl oz/1$^1/2$ cups) lukewarm buttermilk
  (see note)
3 teaspoons salt
polenta, extra
1 egg

Serves 6 as an accompaniment

Mix the yeast with the sugar and a little warm water. Set aside for 30 minutes. If the yeast is not frothy after this time, throw it away and start again.

In the bowl of an electric mixer, combine the flour, polenta and yeast mixture. Add the butter and buttermilk and bring together using a dough hook. You may need to add a little more buttermilk or water. Scrape down the bowl and knead the dough for 10 minutes. Add the salt and knead for a further 5 minutes, or until the dough is smooth. (Alternatively, knead by hand for 5–8 minutes.)

Cover the bowl with plastic wrap and set aside in a warm place for 40–50 minutes, or until the dough has doubled in size.

Preheat the oven to 210°C (415°F/Gas 6–7). Turn the dough out onto a floured surface and knock it back. Shape the dough into a large cob. Transfer the dough to a baking tray lined with baking paper, sprinkle with polenta and set aside to rise for a further 30 minutes.

Beat the egg with a little water to make a glaze. Using a sharp knife, mark a cross on top of the dough, brush with the egg and bake for 15 minutes. Reduce the oven to 180°C (350°F/Gas 4) and bake for a further 20–25 minutes, or until golden.

note
Buttermilk will split very easily if it is boiled or overheated. To heat gently, pour the buttermilk into a bowl over a saucepan of hot water and set aside until just warm.

to drink
Chapel Hill Unwooded Chardonnay, McLaren Vale, South Australia
Australian unwooded chardonnay is smooth and full flavoured. With a ripe, tropical fruit salad structure it has natural food style.

desserts and conversation

The end of a meal can be either the high point or the low point, and often what people will remember most, so do it well.

iced coconut and pineapple terrine with glass biscuits

Coconut sorbet
140 g (5 oz/^{2}/$_3$ cup) caster (superfine) sugar
500 ml (17 fl oz/2 cups) coconut milk
50 g (1^3/$_4$ oz) glucose syrup
juice of 3 limes
grated zest of 1 lime

Pineapple sorbet
200 g (7 oz/scant 1 cup) caster (superfine) sugar
50 g (1^3/$_4$ oz) glucose syrup
juice of 1 lemon
800 ml (28 fl oz/3^1/$_4$ cups) pineapple juice

Glass biscuits
100 g (3^1/$_2$ oz) unsalted butter
175 g (6 oz/heaped ^{3}/$_4$ cup) caster (superfine) sugar
90 g (3^1/$_4$ oz) glucose syrup
90 g (3^1/$_4$ oz/^{3}/$_4$ cup) plain (all-purpose) flour

To serve
200 ml (7 fl oz) coconut cream
100 g (3^1/$_2$ oz/scant ^{1}/$_2$ cup) caster (superfine) sugar
18 lychees, peeled
grated zest of 2 limes

serves 8–10

Line a 20 x 10 cm (8 x 4 inch) loaf tin or a terrine mould with plastic wrap or baking paper, leaving an overhang. To make the coconut sorbet, put the sugar and 100 ml (3^1/$_2$ fl oz) of the coconut milk in a saucepan and stir over low heat until the sugar has dissolved. Add the remaining coconut milk, glucose and lime juice and bring to the boil. Set aside to cool, then churn in an ice cream machine. Fold through the lime zest, then spoon the sorbet into the prepared mould. Freeze while preparing the pineapple sorbet.

To make the pineapple sorbet, put the sugar, glucose, lemon juice and 100 ml (3^1/$_2$ fl oz) of the pineapple juice in a saucepan. Bring to the boil, then simmer for 2–3 minutes. Set aside to cool. Add the remaining juice and churn in an ice cream machine. Spoon the pineapple sorbet over the coconut sorbet to reach the top of the mould. Smooth the top with a metal spoon. Cover with the plastic wrap or baking paper and freeze overnight.

To make the glass biscuits, preheat the oven to 160°C (315°F/Gas 2–3). Gently heat the butter, sugar and glucose in a saucepan until melted. Transfer to a mixing bowl, add the flour and mix. Set aside to cool. Shape the mixture into small marble-sized balls and put on a greased baking tray, leaving 7.5 cm (3 inches) between the balls (the mixture will spread). Bake for 8–10 minutes. Cool the biscuits on the tray for 20–30 seconds, then lift off and drape over a rolling pin to cool. Alternatively, for flat biscuits, allow to cool on the tray.

To make the coconut syrup, put the coconut cream and sugar in a non-stick or stainless saucepan over medium heat. Stir to dissolve the sugar. Remove from the heat and set aside. To turn out the terrine, run the base of the mould briefly under running water, then tap the terrine out onto a tray. Return to the freezer before slicing. To serve, cut the terrine into thick slices and arrange a slice on each serving plate. Place the lychees alongside, spoon coconut syrup over the lychees and finish with grated lime zest. Serve with the glass biscuits.

to drink
Lychee Caprioska
The unique flavour of lychee works wonderfully with vodka and lime and is perfect with the iced terrine. To make, crush 2 lychees with the juice of ^{1}/$_2$ lime. Shake over ice with 30 ml (1 fl oz) each of vodka and lychee liqueur.

iced honey and drambuie parfait with fresh figs

200 g (7 oz/scant 1 cup) caster (superfine) sugar
9 egg yolks
670 ml (22^1/2 fl oz/2^2/3 cups) cream
grated zest of 1 orange
90 g (3^1/4 oz/^{1}/4 cup) honey
80 ml (2^3/4 fl oz/^{1}/3 cup) Drambuie
1 teaspoon natural vanilla extract
6 figs, quartered (see note)
biscotti, to serve (see note)

Cardamom syrup
250 g (9 oz/heaped 1 cup) caster (superfine) sugar
5 cardamom pods, lightly crushed
125 ml (4 fl oz/^{1}/2 cup) fresh orange juice

Serves 6

Line a 32 x 7 cm (12^3/4 x 2^3/4 inch) loaf tin or a terrine mould with plastic wrap, leaving an overhang. Put the sugar and 125 ml (4 fl oz/^{1}/2 cup) water in a saucepan over low heat. Bring to the boil, then reduce the heat and simmer for 5 minutes, or until the syrup reaches soft ball stage — 116°C (240°F) on a sugar thermometer or when a little syrup dropped into a glass of cold water forms a soft ball.

Whisk the egg yolks with electric beaters until thick and pale. With the machine still running, gradually drizzle in the sugar syrup, whisking constantly until the mixture has cooled.

Whip the cream until soft peaks form. Stir the orange zest, honey, Drambuie and vanilla into the cooled egg yolk mixture. Using a whisk, carefully fold through the whipped cream. Pour the parfait mixture into the prepared mould, cover with the overhanging plastic wrap and freeze overnight.

To make the cardamom syrup, put the sugar and 125 ml (4 fl oz/^{1}/2 cup) water in a saucepan over high heat. Cook until the mixture is a dark caramel, taking care not to burn. Remove from the heat and carefully add the cardamom pods and orange juice — the toffee mixture will spit. Return to the heat and stir until the mixture is smooth. Remove from the heat and set aside to cool, then strain.

To serve, run the base of the mould briefly under hot water, then gently tap the parfait out onto a chopping board. Cut the parfait into 1.5 cm (^{5}/8 inch) thick slices with a hot knife. Place two slices of parfait in the centre of each serving plate. Arrange the figs alongside the parfait, then spoon over the syrup. Serve with biscotti.

note
If figs are out of season, the parfait can also be served with other fruit, such as fresh berries or grilled (broiled) peaches. You can use any favourite biscuit instead of the biscotti.

to drink
Knappstein Late Harvest Riesling, Clare Valley, South Australia
To avoid overpowering this dish you need to match it with an elegant, delicate dessert wine. With layers of honey and lime, riesling is just perfect.

coffee crème brûlée

This twist on the classic French crème brûlée comes with a caffeine and liqueur hit —
rich and strong, you won't need to serve coffee afterwards.

30 g (1 oz/^{1}/$_3$ cup) coffee beans
680 ml (23^1/$_2$ fl oz/2^3/$_4$ cups) cream
9 egg yolks
80 g (2^3/$_4$ oz/^{1}/$_3$ cup) caster (superfine) sugar
1^1/$_2$ tablespoons coffee liqueur, such as Tia Maria
caster (superfine) sugar, extra

Serves 6

Preheat the oven to 160°C (310°F/Gas 2–3). To break up the coffee beans, put them in a piece of muslin or a clean tea towel and break up roughly with a meat mallet or rolling pin. Put the broken coffee beans in a large heavy-based saucepan with the cream and bring just to the boil. Remove from the heat and stand for 5 minutes.

Whisk the egg yolks and sugar until thick and pale. Stir through the Tia Maria. Strain the cream through muslin cloth, then slowly pour over the egg mixture and whisk to combine.

Pour the mixture into six 185 ml (6 fl oz/^{3}/$_4$ cup) capacity ramekins. Put the ramekins in a roasting tin and pour enough boiling water into the tin to reach halfway up the sides of the ramekins. Bake the crème brûlée for 20–25 minutes, or until just set. Cool, then refrigerate until completely cold.

To serve, sprinkle the brûlée liberally with the extra caster sugar, cleaning the edges of the ramekins to prevent burning. Using a kitchen blowtorch, or the griller (broiler), caramelize the tops of the brûlée.

note
A grill (broiler) can be used to caramelize the tops of the brûlée, although the brûlée tend to soften before they glaze. Kitchen blowtorches can be purchased from all good kitchenware shops and are a lot more fun!

to drink
Sheridans Liqueur
Coffee and chocolate were made for each other and with this liqueur you virtually have dessert in a glass, as well as on the plate.

buttermilk panna cotta with rhubarb and strawberry soup

3 gelatine leaves (see essentials)
400 ml (14 fl oz) cream
150 g (5^1/2 oz/^{2}/3 cup) caster (superfine) sugar
250 ml (9 fl oz/1 cup) buttermilk
6 strawberries, hulled, halved and thinly sliced
6 basil leaves, finely sliced if large
almond biscotti

Rhubarb and strawberry soup
4 rhubarb stalks, chopped (about 175 g/6 oz)
250 g (9 oz) strawberries, hulled
200 g (7 oz/scant 1 cup) caster (superfine) sugar
5 black peppercorns

Serves 6

Soak the gelatine in cold water to soften. Combine the cream and sugar in a saucepan over medium heat and heat until almost boiling. Transfer to a small bowl.

Remove the gelatine from the water and squeeze out the excess water. Whisk the gelatine into the hot cream mixture until the gelatine has completely dissolved. Stir in the buttermilk, then strain and cool.

Rinse six 125 ml (4 fl oz/^{1}/2 cup) capacity dariole moulds with cold water. Pour the mixture into the moulds and refrigerate overnight.

To make the rhubarb and strawberry soup, put the rhubarb, strawberries, sugar, peppercorns and 1 litre (35 fl oz/4 cups) water in a non-stick or stainless saucepan. Bring to the boil, then reduce the heat and simmer for 20 minutes. Remove from the heat and set aside to infuse for 1 hour.

Strain the soup through a muslin cloth, discarding the fruit and peppercorns. Chill the soup before serving.

To serve, run a knife around the inside of the dariole moulds, then gently shake the panna cotta into the middle of serving bowls. Ladle the soup into the bowls, add the sliced strawberries and sprinkle with the basil. Serve the almond biscotti alongside.

note
You can use metal dariole moulds, but I prefer the little plastic ones (available in commercial stores), as they are pliable. After you've run a knife around the inside of the mould simply squeeze to release the panna cotta.

to drink
Brown Brothers Sparkling Rosé, King Valley, Victoria
This sparkling rosé smells of strawberry and has a palate that is soft, clean and crisp. A lovely choice.

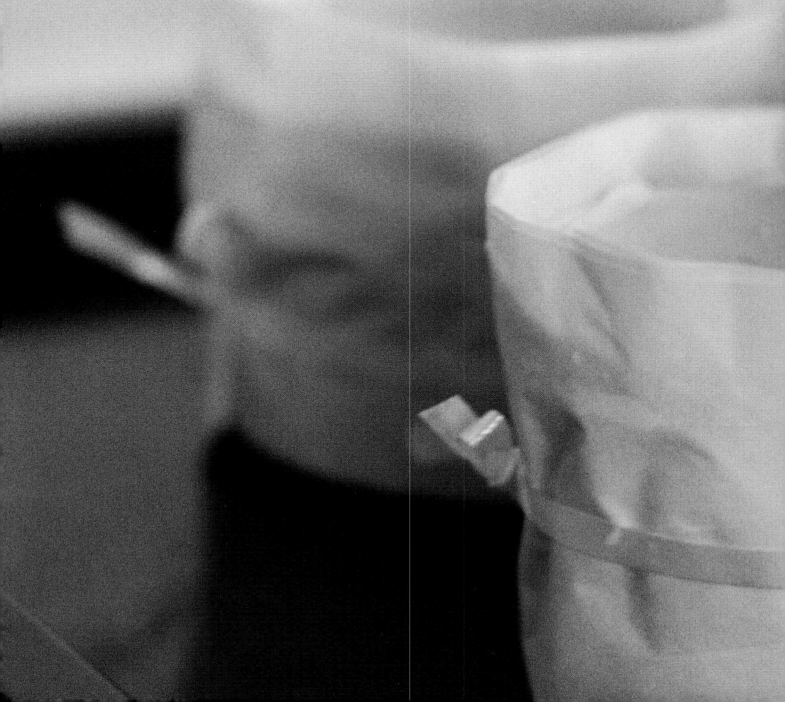
To cook well takes practice and persistence

but, equally, you should just relax and enjoy yourself.

iced orange and cardamom soufflés with citrus salad

140 g (5 oz/^{2}/$_3$ cup) caster (superfine) sugar
6 cardamom pods, cracked
6 egg yolks
450 ml (16 fl oz) cream
1 teaspoon natural vanilla extract
1 tablespoon honey
60 ml (2 fl oz/^{1}/$_4$ cup) Cointreau or
    Grand Marnier
grated zest of 1 orange
candied orange zest (optional)

Citrus salad
2 oranges
2 limes
2 grapefruit
a few mint sprigs, leaves picked and washed (optional)

Makes 6

Measure strips of baking paper to wrap around the outside of six 125 ml (4 fl oz/^{1}/$_2$ cup) capacity ramekins. Secure each strip of paper with a rubber band, allowing the paper to sit 2–3 cm (^{3}/$_4$–1^1/$_4$ inches) above the top of the ramekin.

Put the sugar and 125 ml (4 fl oz/^{1}/$_2$ cup) water in a small saucepan over low heat. Bring to the boil, then add the cardamom pods and simmer for 5 minutes, or until the syrup reaches soft ball stage — 116°C (240°F) on a sugar thermometer or when a little syrup dropped into a glass of cold water forms a soft ball.

Whisk the egg yolks until thick and pale. Strain the sugar syrup, discarding the cardamom pods, and gradually drizzle onto the egg yolks, whisking constantly until combined. Set aside to cool to room temperature.

Whip the cream with the vanilla, honey and Cointreau until soft peaks form. Fold through the orange zest. Fold the whipped cream through the cooled egg yolk mixture.

Pour the soufflé mixture into the prepared ramekins to reach the tops of the paper collars. Freeze overnight, or until set. To make the citrus salad, peel the oranges, limes and grapefruit and cut into segments, slicing between the membranes. Put the segments in a bowl, squeezing in any juice from the remaining pulp. Add the mint, if using.

To serve, remove the soufflés from the freezer 10 minutes before serving. Remove the baking paper and clean the outsides of the ramekins if necessary. Serve with the citrus salad and top with the candied zest, if using.

to drink
Pipers Brook Cuvée Clark Late Harvest Riesling, Tasmania
The cool Tasmanian climate produces dessert wines showing intense candied orange and dried fruits interlaced with honey — the perfect complement to a dessert soufflé.

mango trifle

4 ripe mangoes
470 g (1 lb 1 oz/2 cups) caster (superfine) sugar
6 gelatine leaves (see essentials)
400 ml (14 fl oz) cream, whipped
12–16 savoiardi (sponge finger biscuits)
a small handful of mint, leaves picked, washed
    and chopped

Caramel shards
225 g (8 oz/1 cup) caster (superfine) sugar

serves 6–8

Peel 2 of the mangoes and roughly chop the flesh, reserving the skin and stones. Purée the mango flesh in a food processor. If necessary for a smooth consistency, pass the flesh through a fine sieve into a large bowl.

Put 225 g (8 oz/1 cup) of the sugar and 500 ml (17 fl oz/2 cups) water in a saucepan. Stir to dissolve the sugar, then bring to the boil. Remove from the heat.

Soak the gelatine in cold water until soft, then squeeze out the excess water. Add the gelatine to the hot sugar syrup. Stir into the mango purée until the gelatine has dissolved. Transfer the mixture to a shallow 25 x 30 cm (10 x 12 inch) cake tin and refrigerate overnight, or until the jelly is set.

Put the remaining sugar and 500 ml (17 fl oz/2 cups) water in a saucepan. Stir until the sugar has dissolved, then bring to the boil. Add the reserved mango skin and stones and simmer for 5 minutes. Set aside to cool, then strain.

To make the caramel shards, put the sugar and 80 ml (2^1/2 fl oz/^{1}/3 cup) water in a heavy-based saucepan. Stir until the sugar has dissolved, then bring to the boil, without stirring, and cook until the syrup turns a dark golden colour. Pour the syrup onto a greased or lined baking tray, tilting the tray to coat it with a thin layer of caramel. Set aside to cool, then break into pieces.

To serve, roughly cut the jelly and place in the base of each serving glass. Put a spoonful of whipped cream on top. Gently warm the mango syrup. Dip two savoiardi biscuits per serve into the syrup. Once they have soaked up some syrup, but still have a little texture, crumble them over the cream. Dice the remaining mangoes and combine with the mint. Divide among the serving glasses. Place another spoonful of cream on top and finish with the caramel shards.

note
The trifle can be kept refrigerated, without the caramel shards on top, until required. The caramel shards may begin to dissolve if refrigerated.

to drink
Mount Horrocks Cordon Cut Riesling, Clare Valley, South Australia
This dessert-style riesling maintains intense, crisp floral characteristics.

tiramisu freddo

My friend and London chef Alastair Little wrote in his book Italian Kitchen — recipes from La Cacciata, *that the tiramisu was the 'black forest gateau for the 1990s, naffer than naff, yet somehow delicious'. I hope he approves of this version.*

5 egg yolks
100 g (3¹/2 oz/scant ¹/2 cup) caster (superfine) sugar
250 g (9 oz) mascarpone cheese
250 g (9 oz) good-quality dark chocolate, roughly
    chopped, melted and cooled
250 ml (9 fl oz/1 cup) cream, whipped
125 ml (4 fl oz/¹/2 cup) dark rum
2 egg whites
550 ml (19 fl oz/2¹/4 cups) espresso or strong
    plunger coffee
400 g (14 oz) savoiardi (sponge finger biscuits)
icing (confectioners') sugar or cocoa powder

Serves 8

Whisk the egg yolks and sugar until thick and pale. Stir in the mascarpone until well combined. Stir in the cooled melted chocolate and 60 ml (2 fl oz/¹/4 cup) of the cream, mixing well. Fold in the remaining cream and 1¹/2 tablespoons of the rum. Beat the egg whites until firm peaks form, then fold into the mascarpone mixture.

Grease a shallow 24 cm (9¹/2 inch) springform tin and line with baking paper. Combine the espresso and remaining rum in a bowl. Dip half the savoiardi in the espresso mixture, ensuring they do not become totally saturated. The coffee mixture should soak half way through the biscuits. (Break a piece off one end to check, if unsure.) Arrange in a radial pattern in the base of the tin. Cover with the mascarpone mixture. Dip the remaining savoiardi in the espresso mixture and arrange on top of the mascarpone mixture. Cover with plastic wrap and freeze overnight, or until set.

To serve, cut into wedges and stand at room temperature for 5–10 minutes before serving. Dust with icing sugar or cocoa.

to drink
Cadburys Cream Liqueur
Poured over crushed ice, it's almost like drinking melted chocolate. Very decadent.

figs poached in valpolicella with mascarpone

Ripe, plump figs are a fantastic and versatile fruit that are beautiful fresh or baked, and can be used in sweet or savoury dishes. They also make a great partner to cheese.

750 ml (26 fl oz/3 cups) Valpolicella (see note)
225 g (8 oz/1 cup) caster (superfine) sugar
a few mint sprigs, picked and washed
grated zest of 1 lemon
grated zest of 1 orange
1 vanilla bean, split lengthwise
9 firm ripe figs (see note)
150 g (5$^1/_2$ oz) mascarpone cheese

Puff pastry twists
1 sheet puff pastry
1 egg, lightly beaten
caster (superfine) sugar

Serves 6

To make the puff pastry twists, preheat the oven to 200°C (400°F/Gas 6). Cut the pastry into 10 x 1.5 cm (4 x $^5/_8$ inch) strips. Brush with the beaten egg and sprinkle liberally with caster sugar. Holding each end, twist the pastry strips into a corkscrew. Put the strips on a baking tray lined with baking paper or on a non-stick baking tray. Bake for 8–10 minutes, or until golden.

Combine the Valpolicella, sugar, mint, lemon and orange zest and vanilla bean in a saucepan and bring to the boil. Add the figs and cover with a plate to keep them submerged. Cook for several minutes, until the figs are just beginning to soften. Remove from the heat and set aside to cool in the syrup.

To serve, cut each fig in half lengthwise and arrange three halves on each serving plate. Serve with mascarpone and the puff pastry twists. If you like, reduce the syrup by two-thirds and drizzle it around the figs.

notes
If you cannot find Valpolicella, choose any fruity, light-bodied Italian red wine.
When buying fresh figs, choose fruit with good colour for their particular variety and ones that are plump and free from blemishes. Figs are commonly pale green in colour, though some varieties can be a rich burgundy red. The fruit is ready for eating when it yields to gentle pressure, but beware of overripe fruit. If figs aren't in season, you can poach other fruits such as pears or cherries.

to drink
Morris Liqueur Tokay, Rutherglen, Victoria
This tokay has aromas of burnt toffee and caramel that would make it delightful with figs.

caramelized pineapple, toasted panettone and yoghurt

We are fortunate in Australia to have fruit like pineapple in such abundance — when I worked in London in the 1980s, I saw chefs handling pineapples as if they were an endangered species. Modern varieties are sweet and aromatic, with flesh that melts in the mouth.

225 g (8 oz/1 cup) caster (superfine) sugar
1 ripe medium-sized pineapple, peeled and sliced
2 teaspoons amaretto
500 g (1 lb 2 oz) panettone, cut into wedges
icing (confectioners') sugar
185 g (6½ oz/¾ cup) Greek-style or sheep's milk
   natural yoghurt

Serves 6–8

To caramelize the pineapple, heat a large heavy-based frying pan over medium heat, add the sugar and 125 ml (4 fl oz/½ cup) water and stir until the sugar has dissolved. Increase the heat to high and cook, without stirring, until the caramel just begins to change colour. Reduce the heat to low, carefully add the pineapple slices and cook until they are tender.

Remove the pineapple from the pan and reserve. Carefully add 125 ml (4 fl oz/½ cup) hot water and stir until the caramel is smooth. Add the amaretto and stir through the syrup.

To serve, lightly toast the panettone and dust it with icing sugar. Divide the pineapple among serving plates and add a spoonful of yoghurt. Rest the panettone on top, then drizzle the amaretto sauce over and around.

to drink
Broke Estate Cordon Cut Sauvignon Blanc, Hunter Valley, New South Wales
This dessert could easily be overpowered. An ideal companion would be a late harvest or cordon cut dessert wine such as this.

grilled rum bananas with vanilla ice cream

6 large bananas
90 g (3^1/$_4$ oz/^{1}/$_2$ cup) soft brown sugar
1^1/$_2$ tablespoons grated lemon zest
125 ml (4 fl oz/^{1}/$_2$ cup) dark rum
60 ml (2 fl oz/^{1}/$_4$ cup) lemon juice
125 g (4^1/$_2$ oz) unsalted butter

Vanilla ice cream
300 g (10^1/$_2$ oz/1^1/$_3$ cups) caster (superfine) sugar
12 egg yolks
2 vanilla beans, split lengthwise
500 ml (17 fl oz/2 cups) milk
500 ml (17 fl oz/2 cups) cream

Serves 6

To make the vanilla ice cream, lightly whisk the sugar and egg yolks together in a bowl. Scrape the seeds from the vanilla beans and put them and the beans into a 2 litre (70 fl oz/8 cup) saucepan. Add the milk and cream to the saucepan and heat until almost boiling.

Whisk the hot milk mixture into the egg yolk mixture, then return the mixture to a clean saucepan over medium heat. Stir constantly with a wooden spoon until the custard has thickened and coats the back of the spoon. Do not allow it to boil. Strain the custard through a fine sieve, then refrigerate until cold. Churn the mixture in an ice cream machine, then store in the freezer.

Preheat a barbecue chargrill or ridged grill pan to medium. Carefully slit each unpeeled banana down one side, open it slightly and put it, cut side up, on a sheet of aluminium foil that has been lined with baking paper. Sprinkle the brown sugar and lemon zest into the opening of each banana. Carefully spoon over the rum and lemon juice and dot with the butter.

Wrap the foil loosely around each banana and cook for 10–15 minutes, or until tender. To serve, unwrap and either serve the bananas in the skin or carefully remove from the skin and place on serving plates. Serve with vanilla ice cream.

to drink
Brown Brothers Noble Riesling, King Valley, Victoria
The theme of butterscotch, luscious toffee and caramel continue through both dessert and wine.

baked vanilla ricotta, grilled figs and honey

750 g (1 lb 10 oz/3 cups) ricotta cheese, crumbled
225 g (8 oz/scant 2 cups) icing (confectioners') sugar
2 eggs
1 egg yolk, extra
1 vanilla bean, split lengthwise
9 figs
caster (superfine) sugar
honey

Serves 6–8

Preheat the oven to 160°C (315°F/Gas 2–3). Grease a medium loaf pan, measuring 21.5 x 11.5 cm (8^1/$_2$ x 4^1/$_4$ inches), and line it with baking paper.

Put the ricotta, icing sugar, eggs and egg yolk in a bowl. Scrape the seeds from the vanilla bean into the bowl, discarding the bean. Beat until smooth. Spoon the mixture into the prepared loaf pan. Smooth over the top with the back of a spoon that has been dipped in hot water.

Put the pan in a roasting tin and pour in enough boiling water to reach halfway up the side of the pan. Bake for 30–40 minutes, or until just set when lightly pressed. Remove the pan from the roasting tin and set aside to cool to room temperature before turning out. Turn out onto a board, trim the ends and cut into slices about 1.5 cm (⁵/8 inch) thick.

Cut the figs in half, sprinkle liberally with caster sugar and cook under a hot grill (broiler) until the sugar begins to caramelize.

To serve, place one or two slices of baked ricotta in the centre of each serving plate with 3 fig halves on top. Drizzle the honey over and around.

to drink
Patrizi Moscato d'Asti, Italy
The ricotta and honey are both very rich, so anything too heavy would become sickly; moscato is light, delicate and slightly effervescent. Just perfect.

soft-centred chocolate puddings and pistachio ice cream

140 g (5 oz) unsalted butter

175 g (6 oz) good-quality dark cooking chocolate, roughly chopped

4 eggs

3 egg yolks

125 g (4^1/$_2$ oz/heaped ^{1}/$_2$ cup) caster (superfine) sugar

1^1/$_2$ tablespoons Grand Marnier

1^1/$_2$ tablespoons plain (all-purpose) flour

150 g (5^1/$_2$ oz/1 punnet) raspberries or strawberries

Pistachio ice cream

300 g (10^1/$_2$ oz/1^1/$_3$ cups) caster (superfine) sugar

12 egg yolks

500 ml (17 fl oz/2 cups) milk

500 ml (17 fl oz/2 cups) cream

175 g (6 oz/1^1/$_4$ cups) shelled unsalted pistachios

60 ml (2 fl oz/^{1}/$_4$ cup) Kirsch

Serves 6

To make the pistachio ice cream, lightly whisk the sugar and egg yolks in a bowl. Pour the milk and cream into a 2 litre (70 fl oz/8 cup) saucepan and heat until almost boiling. Whisk the hot milk mixture into the egg yolk mixture, then return the mixture to a clean saucepan over medium heat. Stir constantly with a wooden spoon until the custard has thickened and coats the back of the spoon. Do not allow it to boil. Strain the custard through a fine sieve, then refrigerate until cold.

Blanch the pistachios in boiling water, then drain and rub in a clean tea towel to remove most of the skin. Briefly pulse the pistachios in a food processor until roughly chopped. Stir in the kirsch. Churn the cold ice cream mixture in an ice cream machine. Stir through the pistachio mixture, then freeze until required.

To make the chocolate puddings, liberally spray six 125 ml (4 fl oz/^{1}/$_2$ cup) aluminium dariole moulds, measuring 6 x 6 cm (2 x 2 inches), with non-stick baking spray. Melt the butter and chocolate together in a double boiler. Lightly whisk the eggs, egg yolks and sugar, then add the warm chocolate mixture and the Grand Marnier. Add the flour and stir until just combined. Pour the pudding mixture into the prepared moulds, put the moulds on a tray and refrigerate overnight, or until set.

Preheat the oven to 220°C (425°F/Gas 7) and bake the puddings for 12 minutes, or until the puddings are slightly raised and pulling away from the edges. (If using a fan-forced oven, cook for only 9–10 minutes.) Rest the puddings in the moulds for 2 minutes before turning out. To serve, turn the puddings out onto serving plates. Place a scoop of ice cream to one side and scatter the berries around the plate. The puddings will ooze from the centre when cut.

note
The dariole moulds are also available in stainless steel but the puddings tend to stick, so be warned.

to drink
All Saints Estate Muscat, Rutherglen, Victoria
A decadent dessert needs a decadent drink: deep, luscious and intense.

chocolate fudge self-saucing pudding

I'd probably credit this pudding with being one of my very first recipes and although it's changed a little since those early days, the approach is the same. Mix it up, pour the sauce over the pudding, then go and sit down for 40 minutes. What could be easier?

125 g (4^1/$_2$ oz/1 cup) plain (all-purpose) flour
2 teaspoons baking powder
a pinch of salt
60 g (2^1/$_4$ oz/^{1}/$_4$ cup) caster (superfine) sugar
2 tablespoons cocoa powder
125 ml (4 fl oz/^{1}/$_2$ cup) milk
1 egg, beaten
1 teaspoon natural vanilla extract
2 tablespoons unsalted butter, melted

50 g (1^3/$_4$ oz) good-quality dark chocolate,
    roughly chopped
cream or vanilla ice cream, to serve

Sauce
140 g (5 oz/^{3}/$_4$ cup) soft brown sugar
2 tablespoons cocoa powder
250 ml (9 fl oz/1 cup) hot water

Serves 6

Preheat the oven to 180°C (350°F/Gas 4). Grease a deep 20 cm (8 inch) round pudding bowl.

Sift the flour, baking powder, salt, sugar and cocoa together. Whisk together the milk, egg, vanilla and melted butter. Fold the milk mixture into the dry ingredients, mixing until smooth. Stir in the chopped chocolate and spoon the mixture into the prepared dish.

To make the sauce, combine the brown sugar, cocoa and hot water and gently pour over the pudding. Bake for 40 minutes, or until the pudding has a sponge texture on top with a rich fudge sauce base.

The pudding is best served immediately, with cream or vanilla ice cream alongside.

to drink
Brown Brothers Sparkling Shiraz, King Valley, Victoria
Try this unique Australian sparkling shiraz with dessert; I think you'll be pleasantly surprised.

apple strudel

2 tablespoons unsalted butter

6 Granny Smith apples, peeled, cored and sliced

100 g (3^1/$_2$ oz/scant ^{1}/$_2$ cup) caster (superfine) sugar

100 g (3^1/$_2$ oz/heaped ^{3}/$_4$ cup) raisins,
    roughly chopped

50 g (1^3/$_4$ oz/^{1}/$_3$ cup) pine nuts, roasted

2 tablespoons dark rum

1 teaspoon ground cinnamon

a pinch of freshly grated nutmeg

5 sheets filo pastry

unsalted butter, melted

caster (superfine) sugar, extra

icing (confectioners') sugar

thick (double/heavy) or pouring cream

Serves 8

Heat a large frying pan over medium heat. Add the butter and quickly sauté the apple until slightly softened. Add the sugar, raisins, pine nuts, rum, cinnamon and nutmeg and cook until most of the liquid has evaporated. Spread the apple mixture onto a tray to cool.

Preheat the oven to 180°C (350°F/Gas 4). Lay a sheet of filo on a flat surface and brush with melted butter. Lay another sheet of filo on top and brush with melted butter. Repeat with the remaining pastry. Put the apple mixture in the centre of the filo and roll up to form a strudel, tucking under the ends. The strudel should be about 8 cm (3 inches) wide and 5 cm (2 inches) high when rolled.

Brush the top of the strudel with melted butter and sprinkle with caster sugar. Bake for 20–30 minutes, or until the pastry is golden and crisp. To serve, dust with icing sugar. Cut into slices and serve with cream.

to drink
Sandalford Late Harvest Riesling Verdelho Semillon, Western Australia
The spiced fruit characteristics of both wine and dish are a warm and homely combination.

lemon delicious

5 eggs, separated
170 g (6 oz/^{3}/$_4$ cup) caster (superfine) sugar
50 g (1^3/$_4$ oz) unsalted butter, melted
300 ml (10^1/$_2$ fl oz) milk
3 teaspoons grated lemon zest
80 ml (2^1/$_2$ fl oz/^{1}/$_3$ cup) lemon juice
90 g (3^1/$_4$ oz/^{3}/$_4$ cup) self-raising flour, sifted
80 g (2^3/$_4$ oz/^{1}/$_3$ cup) caster (superfine) sugar, extra
icing (confectioners') sugar
vanilla ice cream

Serves 6

Preheat the oven to 170°C (325°F/Gas 3). Lightly grease a deep 22–24 cm (8^1/$_2$–9^1/$_2$ inch) rectangular or round ovenproof dish.

Whisk the egg yolks and sugar in a large bowl until thick and pale. Beat in the melted butter, milk, lemon zest and lemon juice. Fold in the sifted flour.

Whisk the egg whites in a clean, dry bowl until soft peaks form. Add the extra sugar and whisk until the egg whites are firm. Beat one-third of the meringue into the egg yolk mixture, incorporating well. Gently fold through the remaining meringue.

Spoon the mixture into the prepared dish and place the dish in a roasting tin. Pour in enough boiling water to reach halfway up the sides of the dish. Bake for 35–40 minutes, or until the pudding springs back when tested. The top will be set and golden, while a sauce will form in the bottom of the dish.

Serve the pudding dusted with icing sugar and with a scoop of vanilla ice cream.

to drink
A good-quality Italian Lemoncello, made from the distillation of fresh lemons, served chilled or even over crushed ice would be delightful with this citrus dessert.

mango and ricotta torte with almond praline

Almond praline
225 g (8 oz/1 cup) caster (superfine) sugar
150 g (5^1/$_2$ oz/1 cup) whole blanched almonds

Butter sponge
4 eggs
225 g (8 oz/1 cup) caster (superfine) sugar
125 g (4^1/$_2$ oz/1 cup) plain (all-purpose) flour
1 tablespoon cornflour (cornstarch)
1 teaspoon baking powder
a pinch of salt
60 g (2^1/$_4$ oz) unsalted butter, melted
2 tablespoons milk

Filling
375 ml (13 fl oz/1^1/$_2$ cups) fresh or frozen mango purée
1^1/$_2$ tablespoons cornflour (cornstarch)
1^1/$_2$ tablespoons water
300 g (10^1/$_2$ oz) cream cheese
125 g (4^1/$_2$ oz/1 cup) icing (confectioners') sugar
300 g (10^1/$_2$ oz/1^1/$_4$ cups) fresh ricotta cheese

To assemble
2 mangoes, thinly sliced
185 ml (6 fl oz/^{3}/$_4$ cup) cream, whipped

Serves 10–12

To make the almond praline, lightly grease a baking tray or line a baking tray with baking paper. Put the sugar and almonds in a heavy-based saucepan over very low heat and cook until the sugar has dissolved. Increase the heat and cook until the almonds are roasted and the caramel turns a rich, golden colour. Pour onto the prepared tray, spread out evenly and leave to cool. Once cold, break into pieces and either pound using a mortar and pestle or break up in a food processor using the pulse button.

To make the butter sponge, preheat the oven to 180°C (350°F/Gas 4). Grease a 24 cm (9^1/$_2$ inch) round cake tin and line it with baking paper. Whisk the eggs and sugar in a bowl until thick and pale. Sift together the plain flour, cornflour, baking powder and salt, then fold through the egg mixture. Fold in the melted butter and milk. Pour the mixture into the prepared tin and bake for 10 minutes. Reduce the oven to 160°C (315°F/Gas 2–3) and bake for a further 30–35 minutes, or until a skewer comes out clean when inserted into the sponge, and the sponge springs back when gently pressed. Transfer the cake to a wire rack to cool completely.

To make the filling, put the mango purée in a heavy-based saucepan over medium heat and bring to the boil. Combine the cornflour and water to form a smooth paste, then slowly drizzle into the mango purée. Cook for several minutes, stirring constantly, until the mixture has thickened and the cornflour has cooked out. Set aside to cool. Combine the cream cheese and sugar in a food processor until smooth. Add the ricotta and cooled mango pulp and combine well, using the pulse button.

To assemble, cut the sponge horizontally into 3 layers. Place the bottom layer on a serving plate. Spread half the filling over the sponge and then half the sliced mango. Repeat with another layer of sponge, filling and mango. Top with the last layer of sponge, spread with the whipped cream and sprinkle with the almond praline.

to drink
Rimfire Liqueur Mead, Queensland
This medieval drink made from fermented local honey looks set to make a comeback.

bistro

macadamia and date tart

Sweet shortcrust pastry
150 g (5½ oz) unsalted butter, chopped
100 g (3½ oz/heaped ¾ cup) icing
 (confectioners') sugar
1 egg
250 g (9 oz/2 cups) plain (all-purpose) flour, sifted
1 egg, lightly beaten

Filling
200 g (7 oz) macadamia nuts, roughly chopped
250 g (9 oz) dates, roughly chopped
185 ml (6 fl oz/¾ cup) corn syrup or golden syrup

70 g (2½ oz) unsalted butter, melted
3 eggs
140 g (5 oz/¾ cup) soft brown sugar
125 ml (4 fl oz/½ cup) cream
1½ tablespoons plain (all-purpose) flour, sifted
½ teaspoon mixed spice

To serve
30 g (1 oz/½ cup) shredded coconut, toasted
coconut ice cream (see page 159)
rum caramel (see page 159)

Serves 8–10

To make the sweet shortcrust pastry, cream the butter and sugar in a food processor. Add the egg, mix well, then add the flour and process until the pastry comes together on the blade. Do not overwork. Knead lightly, then wrap in plastic wrap and refrigerate for 1 hour.

Roll out the pastry to a thickness of 3 mm (⅛ inch) and gently ease into a shallow 28 cm (11 inch) round tart tin. Refrigerate or freeze for a further 30 minutes.

Preheat the oven to 180°C (350°F/Gas 4). Line the pastry shell with a piece of baking paper and baking beads (or dried beans or rice). Blind bake the pastry for 20 minutes. Remove the paper and beads and brush the pastry with the beaten egg. Reduce the oven to 160°C (315°F/Gas 2–3) and bake for a further 10 minutes, or until golden. Increase the oven to 170°C (325°F/Gas 3).

To make the filling, combine the macadamia nuts and dates with the corn syrup. Stir through the melted butter. Lightly whisk the eggs, sugar and cream. Fold in the flour and mixed spice, then add to the macadamia mixture. Pour the filling into the pastry shell and bake for 40–50 minutes, or until just set. Cool the tart in the tin before serving.

To serve, place a wedge of tart in the centre of each serving plate, with a spoonful of coconut ice cream alongside and topped with shredded coconut. Drizzle the rum caramel around.

to drink
Petersons Botrytis Semillon, Hunter Valley, New South Wales
You can't get more Australian than macadamia nuts, Bundaberg rum and Hunter Valley semillon.

coconut ice cream

250 g (9 oz/heaped 1 cup) caster (superfine) sugar
10 egg yolks
400 ml (14 fl oz) tin coconut milk
400 ml (14 fl oz) tin coconut cream
30 g (1 oz/$^1/_3$ cup) desiccated coconut, toasted

Serves 6

Lightly whisk the sugar and egg yolks in a bowl. Pour the coconut milk and coconut cream into a large saucepan and heat until almost boiling. Whisk the hot coconut mixture into the egg yolk mixture, then return the mixture to a clean saucepan over medium heat. Stir constantly with a wooden spoon until the custard has thickened and coats the back of a spoon. Do not allow it to boil. Strain the custard through a fine sieve, then refrigerate until cold.

Churn the cold ice cream mixture in an ice cream machine. When half churned, add the toasted coconut and continue to churn. Freeze until required.

rum caramel

125 g (4$^1/_2$ oz/heaped $^1/_2$ cup) caster (superfine)
   sugar
2 tablespoons dark rum
1$^1/_2$ tablespoons cream

Serves 6

To make the rum caramel, combine the sugar and 125 ml (4 fl oz/$^1/_2$ cup) water in a small saucepan. Stir over low heat until the sugar has dissolved. Bring to the boil and cook, without stirring, until the syrup turns a dark caramel colour. Immediately remove from the heat and very carefully stir in the rum — the caramel will spit. Add a little more water if the caramel is too thick. Return to the heat and add the cream. Bring to the boil, then remove from the heat and strain.

There are only a few things to keep in mind when planning

dessert — keep it light, fresh, interesting and seasonal.

pear and frangipane tarts with chocolate sauce

750 g (1 lb 10 oz/3^1/$_4$ cups) caster (superfine) sugar
3 beurre bosc pears
2 sheets puff pastry
1 egg, beaten

Chocolate sauce
125 g (4^1/$_2$ oz) dark couverture chocolate, grated
1^1/$_2$ tablespoons caster (superfine) sugar
60 ml (2 fl oz) cream

Frangipane
50 g (1^3/$_4$ oz) unsalted butter
60 g (2^1/$_4$ oz/^{1}/$_4$ cup) caster (superfine) sugar
1 egg
1^1/$_2$ tablespoons plain (all-purpose) flour, sifted
60 g (2^1/$_4$ oz/^{1}/$_4$ cup) ground almonds (almond meal)

Serves 6

Bring 1 litre (35 fl oz/4 cups) water and the sugar to the boil in a large saucepan. Add the unpeeled pears and cover them with baking paper and a plate to keep them completely submerged during poaching. Poach until tender. Cool the pears in the poaching liquid. Remove the pears from the poaching liquid and drain on paper towels. Cut the pears in half, scoop out the cores and pat dry with paper towels.

To make the chocolate sauce, bring the chocolate, sugar and 300 ml (10^1/$_2$ fl oz/1^1/$_4$ cups) water to the boil in a saucepan, stirring constantly with a wooden spoon. Reduce the heat and simmer gently for 10 minutes, then skim the surface and remove from the heat. Whisk in the cream, then strain and set aside to cool to room temperature.

To make the frangipane, cream the butter and sugar until light and pale. Beat in the eggs. Combine the flour and ground almonds and fold through the butter mixture.

Preheat the oven to 220°C (425°F/Gas 7). Use a pear as a guide to cut the pastry by laying half a pear flat on a sheet of puff pastry and cutting the pastry to a similar shape, allowing a 1.5 cm (^{5}/$_8$ inch) border around the pear. Cut out 6 pastry shapes.

Lay the pastry on a baking tray lined with baking paper. Place 2–3 teaspoons of frangipane in the centre of each piece, lay the poached pear halves on top and brush the outer edges of the pastry with the beaten egg. Bake for 10–15 minutes, or until the pastry is well coloured and slightly risen around the pear.

To serve, drizzle the pears with the chocolate sauce. Store any leftover chocolate sauce and frangipane in the refrigerator.

to drink
Coriole Botrytis Chenin Blanc, McLaren Vale, South Australia
Chenin blanc has delicate flavours of pear and green apple that work well with this dish.

tunisian orange and almond cake

375 g (13 oz) unsalted butter, softened

375 g (13 oz/1²/₃ cups) caster (superfine) sugar

6 eggs

zest of 1 orange

300 g (10¹/₂ oz/2¹/₂ cups) plain (all-purpose)
    flour, sifted

3 teaspoons baking powder

75 g (2¹/₂ oz/²/₃ cups) ground almonds (almond meal)

100 ml (3¹/₂ fl oz) fresh orange juice

2¹/₂ tablespoons extra virgin olive oil

icing (confectioners') sugar, for dusting

natural yoghurt, to serve

Orange syrup

juice of 3 oranges

zest of 2 oranges

juice and zest of 1 lemon

150 g (5¹/₂ oz/²/₃ cup) caster (superfine) sugar

2 cinnamon sticks

2 vanilla beans, split

a few cloves

2 seedless oranges, peeled and cut into rounds

Serves 8–10

Preheat the oven to 170°C (325°F/Gas 3). Grease a 26 cm (10¹/₂ inch) springform tin and line the base with baking paper.

Cream the butter and sugar until light and pale. Add the eggs, one at a time, beating well after each addition. Add the orange zest.

Fold in the sifted flour, baking powder and ground almonds. Fold through the orange juice and olive oil. Spoon the mixture into the prepared tin and bake for 1–1¹/₄ hours, or until cooked when tested. Transfer the cake to a wire rack and cool to room temperature.

To make the orange syrup, put the orange juice and zest, lemon juice and zest, sugar, cinnamon sticks, vanilla beans and cloves in a small saucepan over medium heat. Bring to the boil, then reduce the heat and simmer briefly. Set aside for the flavours to infuse. Add the orange slices and set aside to cool.

Clean the cake tin and re-line it with baking paper. Invert the cake back into the tin so the flat bottom is facing up. Using a wooden or metal skewer, pierce numerous deep holes all over the cake. Gently remove the orange slices from the syrup and set aside. Pour the syrup over the cake. (If making in advance, it can be stored at this point in an airtight container or refrigerated.)

To serve, arrange some orange slices on each serving plate. Top with wedges of cake, dust with icing sugar and serve with yoghurt.

to drink

De Bortoli Noble One Botrytis Semillon, Riverina, New South Wales
The benchmark for Australian dessert wines internationally. It has a palate of apricot and orange marmalade that just has to be mentioned.

espresso cake with kahlua cream and roasted almonds

240 g (8^1/$_2$ oz) unsalted butter, softened
240 g (8^1/$_2$ oz/heaped 1 cup) caster (superfine) sugar
4 eggs
250 g (9 oz/2 cups) plain (all-purpose) flour, sifted
1 teaspoon baking powder
grated zest of 1 lemon
500 ml (17 fl oz/2 cups) hot strong plunger coffee
175 g (6 oz/^{3}/$_4$ cup) caster (superfine) sugar
250 ml (9 fl oz/1 cup) cream
45 ml (1^1/$_2$ fl oz) Kahlua or Tia Maria
roasted flaked almonds

Serves 8

Preheat the oven to 160°C (315°F/Gas 2–3). Grease a 20 cm (8 inch) springform tin or round cake tin and line the tin with baking paper.

Cream the butter and sugar until light and pale, then add the eggs, one at a time, beating well after each addition. Fold in the sifted flour, baking powder and lemon zest. Spoon the mixture into the prepared tin and bake for 1 hour, or until a skewer comes out clean when inserted into the centre. Turn the cake out onto a wire rack to cool completely.

Combine the coffee and sugar and stir until the sugar has dissolved.

Clean the cake tin and re-line it with baking paper. Invert the cake back into the tin so the flat bottom is facing up. Using a wooden or metal skewer, pierce numerous, deep holes all over the cake. Pour the hot coffee syrup over the cake and refrigerate for several hours, or preferably overnight.

To serve, remove the cake from the tin, pierced side up. Whip the cream with the Kahlua, then spread over the cake. Sprinkle with flaked almonds and cut into wedges.

to drink
Espresso cake needs nothing more than a short black coffee and a shot of amaretto served over crushed ice.

flourless pineapple and coconut cake

This cake took a bit of experimentation but you will be glad that we, not you, cooked it a dozen times and worked out that the fruit needed to be cooked first, otherwise the acid in the pineapple caused the cake to collapse!

330 g (11$\frac{1}{2}$ oz) pineapple flesh (about $\frac{1}{2}$ small
   pineapple)
2–3 tablespoons caster (superfine) sugar
250 g (9 oz) unsalted butter, softened
250 g (9 oz/heaped 1 cup) caster (superfine) sugar
6 eggs
200 g (7 oz/2 cups) ground almonds (almond meal)
150 g (5$\frac{1}{2}$ oz/1$\frac{2}{3}$ cups) desiccated coconut
1 tablespoon baking powder, sifted

To serve
80 ml (2$\frac{1}{2}$ fl oz/$\frac{1}{3}$ cup) crème fraîche
250 g (9 oz/1$\frac{1}{2}$ cups) diced pineapple
1 tablespoon picked and washed small mint leaves

Serves 8–10

Preheat the oven to 200°C (400°F/Gas 4). Grease and line a shallow 25 x 30 cm (10 x 12 inch) cake tin.

Finely dice the pineapple flesh or pulse briefly in a food processor, then allow to stand for several minutes in a strainer. Put the diced pineapple in a non-stick frying pan, sprinkle with caster sugar to sweeten, then cook over low heat for several minutes to soften, allowing the pineapple to colour slightly.

Cream the butter and sugar in a mixing bowl. Add two whole eggs and beat well. Separate the remaining eggs. Add the yolks, one at a time, beating well after each addition. Combine the ground almonds, coconut and baking powder and add to the butter mixture alternately with the pineapple.

Whisk the egg whites to soft peaks and carefully fold through the batter. Pour the mixture into the prepared tin and bake for 10 minutes. Reduce the oven to 160°C (315°F/Gas 2–3) and bake for a further 25–30 minutes, or until the cake pulls away from the side of tin. This cake is best served at room temperature and should be stored in an airtight container.

To serve, cut the cake into 7 cm (2$\frac{3}{4}$ inch) squares. Place a spoonful of crème fraîche alongside or on top of the cake. Combine the diced pineapple and the mint and spoon over the cake.

to drink
Bridgewater Mill Sharefarmers Botrytis, Coonawarra, South Australia
The pineapple's sweet acidity cuts through this wine's complex honeyed apricot palate.

buttermilk pancakes with banana, raspberries and maple syrup

250 g (9 oz/2 cups) plain (all-purpose) flour, sifted
a pinch of salt
1 tablespoon baking powder
1 teaspoon bicarbonate of soda
100 g ($3^1/2$ oz/scant $^1/2$ cup) caster (superfine) sugar
500 ml (17 fl oz/2 cups) buttermilk

4 eggs, separated
clarified butter (see essentials)
3 bananas, sliced
150 g ($5^1/2$ oz/1 punnet) raspberries
maple syrup

Serves 6

Preheat the oven to 120°C (250°F/Gas $^1/2$). Combine the flour, salt, baking powder, bicarbonate of soda and sugar in a large bowl, mix well and make a well in the centre. Whisk the buttermilk and egg yolks, then stir into the dry ingredients to form a batter. Whisk the egg whites to soft peaks and fold into the batter.

Preheat a grill (broiler) to medium hot. Brush blini pans with clarified butter (or use a non-stick frying pan) and cook the batter over medium heat until the underside is golden. Put the blini pans under the grill to cook the other side or, if using a frying pan, gently turn the pancakes when bubbles burst on the surface, using a spatula. Keep the pancakes warm in the oven while you cook the remaining batter.

To serve, place two to three pancakes on each serving plate and top with the banana and raspberries. Drizzle with maple syrup and serve immediately.

to drink
Catherine Blossom Cocktail
Fresh orange, a dash of maple syrup and a little lime make this drink a great way to start the day. To make, process 6–8 ice cubes, 250 ml (9 fl oz/1 cup) fresh orange juice, 1 tablespoon maple syrup and a dash of lime juice in a blender in short bursts. Serve garnished with a twist of lime.

hot cross buns

160 g (5³/4 oz/1 cup) raisins, roughly chopped

115 g (4 oz/³/4 cup) currants

grated zest of 1 orange

100 ml (3¹/2 fl oz) fresh orange juice

1 tablespoon dried yeast

60 ml (2 fl oz/¹/4 cup) warm water

185 ml (6 fl oz/³/4 cup) warm milk

1 teaspoon natural vanilla extract

125 g (4¹/2 oz) unsalted butter, melted

90 g (3¹/4 oz/¹/2 cup) soft brown sugar

1 teaspoon ground cinnamon

1 teaspoon ground nutmeg

625 g (1 lb 6 oz/5 cups) plain (all-purpose) flour, sifted

1 teaspoon allspice

3 eggs

1 teaspoon salt

60 g (2¹/4 oz/¹/2 cup) plain (all-purpose) flour, extra

To glaze

115 g (4 oz/¹/2 cup) caster (superfine) sugar

Makes 12

Soak the raisins, currants and orange zest in the orange juice overnight.

Preheat the oven to 170°C (325°/Gas 3). Combine the yeast and warm water and set aside for 15 minutes. If the yeast is not frothy after this time, throw it away and start again.

Combine the warm milk, vanilla, butter, sugar, cinnamon and nutmeg in a large bowl. Combine the sifted flour with the allspice. Stir the yeast mixture and 375 g (13 oz/3 cups) of the flour mixture into the milk mixture and beat to combine. Add the eggs, one at a time, then mix in the remaining flour mixture, salt and soaked fruit.

Using a dough hook, knead the mixture for 10 minutes, or until springy to touch. (Alternatively, knead by hand for 5–8 minutes.) The mixture will be quite tacky. Transfer to an oiled bowl, cover with plastic wrap and set aside to rise for 1 hour.

Divide the mixture into 12 pieces. Using a little flour and the palm of your hand, roll to form each piece into a smooth ball. Put the balls on a greased baking tray, cover with a damp cloth and set aside in a warm place to prove for a further 30 minutes.

Mix the extra flour with 100–125 ml (3¹/2–4 fl oz) water to form a thick paste. Pipe a cross onto each bun. Bake the hot cross buns for 35–40 minutes. To make the glaze, put the sugar and 125 ml (4 fl oz/¹/2 cup) water into a pan and bring to the boil. Stir until the sugar dissolves. Brush over the buns for the last 5 minutes of baking.

to drink

Grecian Coffee

A couple of buns, a nice warming liqueur coffee and maybe a couple of Easter eggs — my wife would be in heaven. To make, pour 3 teaspoons amaretto, 3 teaspoons Metaxa (a well-known Greek brandy, or use a similar quality brandy) and freshly brewed coffee into a liqueur coffee or tall glass. Top with whipped cream and chocolate shavings.

panforte

Panforte looks exotic, and it is, but it's not that hard to prepare and it makes a wonderful gift, if you spend a little effort on the packaging. In this age of ready-made everything, a hand-made gift seems such a special thing.

150 g (5¹/2 oz) hazelnuts, roasted, skinned and
    roughly chopped
150 g (5¹/2 oz) whole blanched almonds, roasted
150 g (5¹/2 oz/1¹/4 cups) raisins
150 g (5¹/2 oz/³/4 cup) mixed peel
100 g (3¹/2 oz) crystallized ginger, roughly chopped
90 g (3¹/4 oz/³/4 cup) plain (all-purpose) flour
2 teaspoons cocoa powder

2 teaspoons ground cinnamon
¹/2 teaspoon allspice
¹/2 teaspoon ground nutmeg
a pinch of ground white pepper
175 g (6 oz/³/4 cup) caster (superfine) sugar
125 g (4¹/2 oz/¹/2 cup) honey
icing (confectioners') sugar (optional)

Makes 20–24 wedges

Preheat the oven to 160°C (315°F/Gas 2–3). Line the base of a 24 cm (9¹/2 inch) springform tin with baking paper and grease the side.

Combine the nuts, raisins, mixed peel, ginger, flour, cocoa and spices in a large bowl.

Put the sugar and honey in a heavy-based saucepan over low heat until the sugar has dissolved. Bring to a simmer and cook until the syrup reaches soft ball stage — 116°C (240°F) on a sugar thermometer or when a little syrup dropped into a glass of cold water forms a soft ball.

Fold the syrup into the dry ingredients, combining well. The mixture will be very tacky. Smooth the mixture into the prepared tin and bake for 35 minutes, or until set. Set aside to cool in the tin.

Turn the panforte out of the tin and wrap in baking paper, then aluminium foil. It will stay moist for at least a month. To serve, cut the panforte into thin wedges and dust with icing sugar.

to drink
Sandalford Sandalera, Margaret River, Western Australia
If I were to describe this interesting drink it would sound remarkably similar to panforte; nutty, with hints of chocolate, honey and spice.

cinnamon and fig turkish delight

65 g (2¼ oz) gelatine powder
680 g (1 lb 8 oz) caster (superfine) sugar
1 teaspoon ground ginger
1 teaspoon ground cinnamon
100 g (3½ oz) dried figs, chopped

50 g (1¾ oz) crystallized ginger, chopped
2 teaspoons rosewater
a few drops of pink food colouring (optional)
icing (confectioners') sugar

Makes 25 pieces

Pour 600 ml (20 fl oz/2½ cups) water into a saucepan. Sprinkle the gelatine over the water and cook over low heat until the gelatine has dissolved. Add the sugar and stir until the mixture is clear. Add the ground ginger and cinnamon, increase the heat to medium and boil for 10–15 minutes, or until syrupy. Remove from the heat and stir in the figs, crystallized ginger and rosewater. Add the food colouring, one drop at a time, if using.

Pour the mixture into an 18 cm (7 inch) square cake tin that has been rinsed with cold water and leave to set overnight (do not cover or refrigerate the mixture). To serve, turn the Turkish delight out onto a board, cut it into small triangles or squares and roll in icing sugar.

note
Turkish delight is best served the next day. When ready to serve, it will be easier to cut if you use a knife that has been dipped in hot water (and wiped dry before cutting). Turkish delight will keep for 2 to 3 weeks stored in an airtight container.

to drink
Capercaillie Gewürztraminer, Hunter Valley, New South Wales
Turkish delight *is* gewürztraminer, with its floral characteristics of sweet lychee and rose petals.

golden fudge

500 g (1 lb 2 oz/4 cups) icing (confectioners') sugar
250 ml (9 fl oz/1 cup) milk
4 tablespoons condensed milk
2 tablespoons golden syrup or maple syrup
2 tablespoons unsalted butter
icing (confectioners') sugar, extra, for dusting (optional)

Makes about 30 pieces

Put the sugar, milk, condensed milk, golden syrup and butter in a heavy-based or non-stick saucepan over low–medium heat. Whisk to combine and dissolve the sugar. Bring to the boil, then reduce the heat to low and simmer for 15 minutes, or until it begins to change colour. (If you have a sugar thermometer, the temperature should be 110–115°C/230–239°F.)

Remove the fudge from the heat and pour into a heatproof bowl. Whisk until the mixture just begins to thicken.

Pour the fudge into a greased 15 x 23 cm (6 x 9 inch) lamington or loaf tin and press into the tin with the back of a metal spoon. Leave to set. To serve, cut the fudge into wedges and dust with icing sugar, if using.

to drink
Nothing beats a hot milky latte and a piece of freshly-made fudge ... other than a hot milky latte and two pieces of freshly-made fudge.

There are a few people who don't have a sweet tooth

— *but not many!*

chocolate and cointreau truffles

100 ml (3$^{1}/_{2}$ fl oz) cream
600 g (1 lb 5 oz) best-quality dark couverture
    chocolate, chopped
150 g (5$^{1}/_{2}$ oz) unsalted butter, roughly chopped
45 ml (1$^{1}/_{2}$ fl oz) Cointreau or Grand Marnier
grated zest of 1 orange
125 g (4$^{1}/_{2}$ oz/1 cup) cocoa powder
60 g (2$^{1}/_{4}$ oz/$^{1}/_{2}$ cup) icing (confectioners') sugar

Makes 25–30 truffles

Put the cream in a small saucepan and bring to the boil. Remove from the heat and set aside to cool. Melt half the chocolate in a double boiler. Pour the cooled cream onto the melted chocolate and whisk until well combined. Set aside to cool to room temperature.

Beat the butter with electric beaters until pale and light. With the machine running, slowly pour in the cooled chocolate mixture, then add the Cointreau and orange zest.

Using a melon baller, shape the truffles into balls (alternatively you could use a piping bag) and place on a tray lined with baking paper. Refrigerate for several hours, or until set.

Sift the cocoa and icing sugar together into a shallow tray. Melt the remaining chocolate in a double boiler. Using a fork, dip the truffles into the chocolate, one at a time, then drop into the cocoa mixture. Once you have 3 or 4 truffles in the cocoa mixture, gently shake the tray or spoon over the cocoa mixture until they are completely covered.

When the chocolate has set (this will take several minutes), use a clean fork to lift the truffles onto a wire rack, allowing the excess cocoa to fall off. Store the truffles in an airtight container in the refrigerator.

note
Truffles are best eaten once they have been at room temperature for 30 minutes as the chocolate coating will still be firm but the inside will be soft.

to drink
The perfect way to finish a great meal. The only addition perhaps being a short black and Cointreau on ice.

frangelico rosso

This is a lovely late afternoon drink, refreshing and indulgent.

Build 2 tablespoons Frangelico, 1^1/$_2$ tablespoons fresh lime juice, 3 teaspoons Campari or Aperol and 1^1/$_2$ tablespoons blood orange juice in a tumbler over ice. Serve with blood orange slices and a wedge of lime. Serves 1

affogato al caffe and frangelico

An affogato is the Italian version of iced coffee, one that has been adopted enthusiastically in Australia. The idea with an affogato (and it doesn't necessarily need to be served with a liqueur) is to pour a shot of espresso coffee and liqueur over the ice cream. The affogato can be sipped slowly or eaten with a spoon and is a great way to enjoy dessert, coffee and an after-dinner drink all in one. They can also be served with biscotti.

Place 2 scoops of vanilla ice cream in a small serving glass with 1 shot of espresso and 1 shot of frangelico (about 1 tablespoon) served separately. Drink the frangelico neat or pour it over the coffee and ice cream. Serves 1

glossary

Al dente
An Italian term literally translated as 'firm to the bite', meaning, cooked until barely tender and retaining some resistance in the centre. It is used to describe cooked pasta and risotto.

Butterfly
To debone and flatten a gamebird, such as quail, and then open out like the wings of a butterfly. If boned and butterflied birds aren't available, buy whole birds and ask the butcher to halve the bird and remove the backbone and ribcage.

Deglaze
The action of adding stock, wine or water to a hot pan after browning the ingredients. This incorporates any solids remaining in the pan into the liquid, which is then added to the dish, providing added flavour.

Dice
To chop into small, even cubes.

Fold
To gently incorporate ingredients with a lifting and cutting action to avoid loss of aeration.

Julienne
To cut into matchstick-sized strips.

Pin-bone
To remove the bones from fish such as salmon, using either salmon tweezers or small electrical pliers available from electrical stores.

Poach
A gentle method of cooking food in barely simmering water or stock.

Purée
To process food in a blender or pass it through a mouli or a sieve, so that no solids remain.

Refresh
To quickly chill blanched vegetables or salad leaves by plunging into iced water.

Roast nuts
Nuts are best roasted by placing them on a baking tray in a preheated 180°C (350°F/Gas 4) oven and cooking until golden. Different varieties roast at different times.

Roast or grill (broil) bacon, pancetta, prosciutto
Preheat the oven to 190°C (375°F/Gas 5). Put the sliced meat in a single layer on a greased or baking paper-lined oven tray and roast in the oven until crisp. Meat may also be grilled (broiled) until crisp.

Sauté
To toss in a small amount of fat (butter or oil) over high heat.

Score
To make shallow incisions on the skin or outer layer of an ingredient to aid cooking.

Seal
To quickly cook food (usually meat) on both sides over very high heat, and thereby seal in the juices.

Sear
To cook very quickly over fierce heat.

Simmer
To heat to just below boiling point. The surface of the liquid should ripple but the bubbles should not break the surface.

Sweat
To cook gently over medium heat; no colour should develop.

essentials

key ingredients

Gelatine
Half a teaspoon of gelatine powder equals 1 gelatine leaf. Dissolve the powder in an equal amount of cold water. This will form a jelly that can then be added to hot liquid, as you would with the leaves. Leaf gelatine is available from good delicatessens and food emporiums, and is considered superior to gelatine powder. I use thin leaf gelatine (gold quality).

Herbs
All our recipes use fresh herbs. Prepare by removing leaves, discarding any that are wilted or damaged. Wash in copious amounts of water and dry in a salad spinner or clean tea towel.

Salad leaves
Always wash salad leaves in copious amounts of cold water allowing any grit to fall to the bottom. Pick out old, damaged or tough sections/stalks. Place the remaining leaves in a salad spinner or clean tea towel to dry. Transfer the dry salad leaves to a large kitchen bowl and dress just before serving. This ensures an even coating of dressing.

Seasonings
Checking and adjusting seasonings refers to tasting a dish and deciding whether or not it requires further flavouring generally with salt or pepper, but it could also refer to checking for sweetness or acidity in dressings. I always use good quality sea salt flakes (such as Maldon) and freshly ground black pepper in both cooking and seasoning.

Spices
I always use whole spices and roast and grind them as required. All spices should be purchased and stored whole, and separately roasted in a dry frying pan until fragrant. Grind to a powder using a mortar and pestle or coffee grinder.

equipment

Dariole moulds
Round, flat-bottomed, metal cups with flared sides, 125 ml (4 fl oz/$1/2$ cup) capacity. They are available in aluminium, stainless steel and plastic. The plastic ones are good for puddings such as panna cotta, as their flexibility makes it easier to turn out the dessert.

Mandolin
Stainless steel manual slicing utensil. Use for very finely slicing any firm fruits or vegetables.

Ramekins
Refers to a ceramic pot used in baking. Ramekins are available in various sizes but they are more commonly recognized as a small soufflé dish, about 8–10 cm ($3^{1}/4$–4 inches) in diameter.

Springform tins
Circular metal cake tins with removable base that are held together by an expanding clamp on the side. They are available in various diameters, generally 6 cm ($2^{1}/2$ inches) high.

Terrines
A lidded dish, of 1.2 litre (42 fl oz) capacity, 25 cm (10 inches) long and 7 cm ($2^{3}/4$ inches) high. Mostly made of cast iron; I recommend Le Creuset.

techniques

Blanching tomatoes
Cut a crisscross in the base of the tomato, dip briefly in boiling water, then refresh in ice water — the skin should peel off easily. Cut and deseed if necessary.

Clarified butter
Clarified butter is butter that has had the milk solids removed, enabling it to be heated to a much higher temperature than regular butter without burning.

To clarify butter, put 250 g (9 oz) butter in a small saucepan over low heat and allow to melt and separate. Carefully pour off the melted butter into a bowl, leaving the milk solids behind. Discard the milk solids and refrigerate the clarified butter.

Jus
Jus is simply reduced stock or an unthickened meat sauce. Good delicatessens and some restaurants sell jus (as well as demi-glace and veal glaze), but you can also prepare your own.

Bring 4 litres (140 fl oz/16 cups) beef stock to the boil over medium heat. Continue to boil until the stock is reduced by two-thirds, occasionally skimming the surface of impurities. The resulting sauce should be thick and glossy.

If, after obtaining the required flavour, the jus is still not of coating consistency, it can be lightly thickened with arrowroot. Combine 3 tablespoons arrowroot with 2 tablespoons cold water, then gradually drizzle just enough into the boiling stock, whisking constantly until the sauce coats the back of a spoon. Strain while hot, cool, then store in a small container in the refrigerator, or freezer for later use.

Salted lemons
Salted lemon is used to enhance seafood dishes, couscous or Moroccan-style foods. The skin of traditionally preserved lemons needs to be thoroughly washed before use, as it is much saltier than the skin of lemons salted using this method.

To make, arrange 4 lemons snugly in a saucepan. Add 125 g (4^1/$_2$ oz/1 cup) sea salt and enough water to cover the lemons. Invert a small plate over the lemons to keep them submerged. Bring to the boil, then reduce the heat and simmer for 20 minutes, or until the rinds are soft. Drain and cool the lemons before storing them in a covered container in the refrigerator for up to two weeks. To use the salted lemons, cut into quarters, scrape out and discard the flesh, then finely dice the rind or cut into thin strips.

Sugar syrup
To make, put 185 ml (6 fl oz/^{3}/$_4$ cup) water, and 125 g (4^1/$_2$ oz/^{1}/$_2$ cup) caster (superfine) sugar into a saucepan over medium heat. Stir to dissolve the sugar. Bring to the boil and simmer for 2 minutes. Remove from the heat, cool completely and strain.

index

190